I MUST BE
DREAMING

LEON NACSON

Newleaf

Newleaf
an imprint of
Gill & Macmillan Ltd
Goldenbridge
Dublin 8
with associated companies throughout the world

First published in Australia by Pan Macmillan Australia Pty Limited.

© Leon Nacson 1997

0 7171 2782 6

Printed by ColourBooks Ltd, Dublin

A catalogue record is available for this book from the British Library.

1 3 5 4 2

Disclaimer

The author of this book does not dispense medical advice or prescribe the
use of any technique as a form of treatment for physical or medical problems
without the advice of a physician, either directly or indirectly. The intent of
the author is only to offer the information of a general nature to help you in
your quest for emotional well-being and good health. In the event you use
any of the information in this book for yourself, which is your right, the
author and the publisher assume no responsibility for your action.
Every attempt has been made to identify and contact owners of copyright for
permission to reproduce material in this book. However, any copyright
holders who have inadvertently been omitted for acknowledgments and
credits should contact the publishers. Any omissions will be rectified in
subsequent editions. Every attempt has been made by the publisher to ensure
that the information in this book is correct at the time of publication.

PREFACE

You can ask anyone and they'll tell you, 'Leon's a Dreamer'. Well I suppose that helps if I'm going to revise and update my first book, *A Dreamer's Guide to the Galaxy*. What also helps is that during my waking life, in between dreams and daydreams, as publisher of *The Planet* newspaper and author and publisher of a number of self help books, I've worked with some of the most inspirational and creative thinkers in the world.

By communicating with these individuals and many others, I have developed some user-friendly concepts that you may find enlightening.

The basic premise of this book is that it's possible to have instant coffee, instant noodles and instant enlightenment. You don't have to eat alfalfa sprouts for twelve months, sacrifice a hippopotamus every Tuesday, deprive yourself of earthly pleasures or go on a quest for the Grail to reach enlightenment. You can if you want to, but I believe that enlightenment is any experience of expanding or contracting your consciousness beyond its present state.

Enlightenment is basically a deeper understanding of one's self. But like your fitness or education, you really are never at the point where you can no longer develop and grow. It is a continuum. There is always something new to learn and experience. Yet with enlightenment we can go two steps forward then one step back. This is part and parcel of the whole deal. It's quite natural to take one step back because with your experience comes doubt; that is, you immediately begin to analyse and intellectualise the little drop of enlightenment you just caught. Enlightenment comes and then you lose sight of it for a while. Just take one step at a time, and realise that the further you go, the easier it becomes to take the next step.

Some people who hear these words may think, 'What! It's that simple? There's got to be more! Don't I have to sit on a hill in Tibet in my birthday suit, first?' I believe, and all the individuals I've worked with in the field of personal growth agree, enlightenment is available to each and every one of us at the snap of a finger.

I believe that dream interpretation is the most personally relevant way of turning on the tap that I call instant enlightenment. Our dreams are laid out before us, there is no effort in bringing their effect into our lives, yet the potential they have to awaken new depths of consciousness dwelling within us is infinite.

ACKNOWLEDGEMENTS

Before I go further, I believe it is appropriate to acknowledge some of the most creative thinkers I have been privileged to work with over the years. Glynn Braddy, Deepak Chopra, Karen Downes, Wayne Dyer, Louise Hay, Marshall N. Lever, Denise Linn, David A. Phillips, Trevor Ravenscroft, Stuart Wilde and Judith White. If you are not familiar with their work, a short synopsis and a contact for each of them has been included at the back of the book.

And it would be remiss of me not to mention the editorial team who have rolled up their sleeves and made this book possible. They include Kim Cotton, Rachel Eldred, Jenny Moalem, Leigh Robshaw, Arthur Stanley and Dr Kal Thomas for running his astute medical eye over the book. Finally, my dearest friends at Pan Macmillan, Amanda Hemmings and Catherine Proctor.

I dedicate this book to my parents,
Eli and Victoria Nacson.
I opened my eyes and you were there.

CONTENTS

INSIGHTS BY
DEEPAK CHOPRA

The evening sun was setting across the horizon in a glow of massive red fire that would evoke blazing passion in anyone's heart. I looked out the window of the library of my hotel in Delhi and was overawed by the scene. I had just ordered a cup of chai tea and my mind began to drift back to the reason why I was there. Deepak Chopra's daughter, Mallika, had just been married and I was fortunate enough to have been invited to participate in the seven-day celebration.

It had been an incredible affair with over one thousand people flying in from all over the world to converge on a farm called The Little Kingdom, just outside Delhi.

The culmination of the event had taken place the evening before. The groom had arrived on an elephant lavishly decorated with paintings, silks and jewels. The ornate saris worn by women from both the East and West swished around me in a rich kaleidoscope of colour. It was an incredibly majestic celebration; spiritual and awesome yet also familiar and homely.

Deep in thought in the hotel room, I looked up and Deepak was standing next to me. I hadn't even heard him come in, I had been blissfully daydreaming. He sat down next to me and we began talking about the fun we had had over the week. Our conversation crossed a number of subjects until we arrived at books we had both written. Deepak then asked me if I had ever considered reprinting or updating my first dream book, *A Dreamer's Guide to the Galaxy*. I replied that I was actually in the process of doing just that. *I Must Be Dreaming* was to be the revised, updated and 'that's it, I'm not touching it again' edition. He then asked me if I had ever considered putting the section 'The Secrets of Sound Sleep' at the front of the book, 'How are you ever going to get good dreams if you don't get a good night's sleep?'

Deepak has a brilliant knack of stating the obvious. I mean it's so simple. How can your dreams be developed, nurtured and even recalled unless the theatre of your dreams, your body and mind, is properly rested? Deepak, having already written a number of books on the subject then began discussing with me his concepts and research concerning the benefits of sleep upon our health. 'Hang on a minute, buddy!' I exclaimed and quickly ran back to my room to get my tape recorder. It was a great opportunity to get the professional opinion on a good night's sleep of one of the most profound medical experts and authors on mind/body health on the planet. The sun had dipped preparing for the evening's entrance as I arrived back armed with my trusty Walkman. It was the perfect moment to talk about the gift of sleep.

So dreamers, what you are now about to read is the conversation I had with Deepak about the best way to get forty winks.

Deepak, I have always believed sleep to be as important to our survival as the air we breathe. What do you think?
The fundamental purpose of sleep is to allow the body to repair and rejuvenate itself. The deep rest provided during sleep allows the body to recover from fatigue and stress and enlivens the body's own self repair and homeostatic, or balancing, mechanisms.

And dreaming? I also consider it to be as vital as sleep.
Yes, I believe it is. Dreaming is a further elaboration of this

process of purifying and cleansing stress and tension from the nervous system. Studies on sleep and dream deprivation strongly support these theories.

Getting back to sleep, so many people today have trouble getting restful sleep on a regular basis. Do you feel this is because of the stresses associated with modern day living?
Let me tell you about an insight that was given to me by one of my patients, a woman who had been deeply troubled by chronic insomnia. I think it will be very useful in explaining why I believe we are a society of troubled sleepers.

For years my patient had lain awake trying to sleep. Then, late one night, she had an important realisation about the source of her insomnia which she shared with me: there were things left undone in her waking life that made her, unconsciously, uncomfortable with going to sleep. There were things she knew she wanted to do — like travelling, getting in touch with an old friend — but they were not things she could simply jump out of bed and take care of on the night of her realisation. They required a long-term reorientation of her life. Once she began that process, her sleep improved because her waking life had improved.

The message here is that millions of us lie awake at night worrying — mentally balancing our cheque books, replaying arguments and misunderstandings — and sleep escapes us.

So you're saying sleep problems often manifest because, for some, life can get out of balance?
This is often the case, yes. Sleep is one of the pillars of health. When sleep is disturbed, it represents a basic disruption of physiological stability. In short, many of the health problems we

experience today—and sleeplessness, or insomnia, is one such complaint—come about because our lives have got out of balance with nature's rhythm. Sleep is most definitely one of those rhythmic cycles we need to stay in touch with. Living in harmony with natural rhythms allows a free passage of biological information and intelligence, while living in opposition to those rhythms fosters disorders at the molecular level and discomfort at the level of everyday experience. Sleep is simply a naturally existing state of consciousness that should come in its own proper cycle day after day, year after year. It's the period of rest where rejuvenation and healing take place.

So, if we want to reap the physical and spiritual benefits of sound sleep and dream states, we need to look after our general health and live in accordance with nature?

It is the only way because in reality there is nothing we can do to force ourselves to sleep. We cannot will sleep. We cannot command sleep. Sleep is a natural process and 'trying' will have no positive effect. Indeed, trying will probably only aggravate insomnia because the harder you try and the less successful you are, the more frustrating the whole thing becomes. There is a very profound reason for this: trying is not the way nature functions. The earth doesn't try to go around the sun, nor does the seed try to sprout into a sapling.

So you're saying that the concept of loosening up and not worrying about it is the best approach to take?

The best thing we can do to promote better sleep once we get into bed is what I call 'not minding'. Nature functions with effortless ease, invariably taking the path of least resistance. This is the principle of least action and maximum efficiency, and it's the one to use when we want to fall asleep. We should just rest comfortably, not minding, and place ourselves in nature's hands. Simply lie in bed with your eyes closed, not minding whether you're awake or asleep. The mere act of remaining motionless with your eyes closed, even if you're feeling anxious or restless, actually provides the body with significant benefits. Go to bed at a regular time, and well before midnight if at all possible. Once in bed assume a comfortable position and don't worry about sleeping. Let your mind wander freely. Take the attitude that you will get as much sleep as nature wants you to have at that moment. You are in nature's hands. Unplug your reading lamp, turn your clock to the wall, don't be concerned about the time. Just enjoy resting comfortably. Sleep will come naturally when it comes, and meanwhile, you're gaining the benefit of valuable rest and rejuvenation of your whole system.

You mean less tossing and turning and more curling up?
There is an old Ayurvedic saying: 'Sleep is the nurse of all living beings.' Sometimes repair is overdue. Perhaps a great deal of stress has accumulated and now needs to be released during the night. This repair work, or release of stress, can increase mental and physiological activity, which may be experienced as physical discomfort, racing thoughts or feelings of anxiety. If this happens, we should realise these sensations of restlessness are a by-product of nature's repair work and try not to resist them.

What are a few pointers to assist those interested in improving the quality of their sleep?
We can restore balance through meditation and emotional poise,

Deepak Chopra

I remember as a child dreaming that I was walking through a forest. As I walked, forest animals began approaching me. I soon found that I could understand the meaning of every sound they made and they could comprehend my words. We conversed until I woke up.

diet and exercise. Meditation gets us in touch with our true selves. Meditation is not really forcing your mind to be quiet; it's finding the quiet that's already there. Behind the screen of our internal dialogue, there is something entirely different: the silence of a mind that is not imprisoned by the past. That's the silence we want to bring into our awareness through meditation. Why is this important? Because silence is the birthplace of happiness. Silence is where we get our bursts of inspiration, our tender feelings of compassion and empathy, our sense of love.

Are there any other simple techniques that you can quickly suggest to improve the quality of our sleep?
There are some techniques I call Body Intelligence Techniques designed to promote restful sleep on a regular basis. I'll list these for you:

- Go to bed at the same time every night, ideally before 10 p.m.
- If you can't fall asleep straight away, adopt the 'not minding' attitude we have already spoken about.
- Eat dinner early in the evening, between 5.30 p.m. and 7 p.m. if possible.
- Take a short five to 15 minute stroll after dinner to help you digest and relax.
- Avoid exciting, dynamic or focused work in the evening.
- Avoid too much TV in the evening. You might like to try light reading, listening to music, playing with the children, having friends over or other relaxed and entertaining activities.
- Begin to prepare for sleep at least 30 minutes before you intend to get into bed.
- Rise at the same time most days. Ideally, you should get up by 6 a.m. (at the latest by 7 a.m.), even on weekends and

holidays. This will help you reset your biological clock. If you need to catch up on sleep, you can always have a light nap later in the day.

✠ Meditation has been around for some time now. In their zeal, scientists have coined some unfortunate terms about meditation, such as 'the relaxation response'. This term really doesn't do justice to meditation. The ancient seers who described the techniques of meditation were not trying to relax—they were quite relaxed already. Meditation was done to experience the state of heightened awareness. During meditation, one elicits not a relaxation response, but a restful alertness response. We meditate not to tune out, but to tune in; not to get away from it all, but to get in touch with it all; not to experience drowsiness, but an inner wakefulness, an inner knowingness that gives us a sense of control over the processes inside our body, as well as over our life experiences.

In the silence of meditation, there is not just relaxation, but alertness, sensitivity, freshness, flexibility, creativity. There is aliveness, there is renewal, there is unbounded energy. In this experience of pure consciousness, there is no contamination by memories, by cravings. Awareness remains pure, full of energy, full of clarity.

Deepak, you've personally taught me Primordial Sound Meditation. Can you give an overview of what makes it so special.

Primordial Sound Meditation (PSM) originated in India and has been practised for thousands of years. It doesn't relate to activity within the mind, its aim is to get to the level of the spirit—or firstly, to the level of the individual soul which is part of the same continuum.

PSM assists you to get in touch with your essential nature, the self behind all the activities of life. It is a technique that allows us to take our awareness from the level of daily actions to a level of silence within.

I call this silence the 'gap'. It is that space between our thoughts. One thought is activity and the next thought is activity, and between these two thoughts is a space where you are having the thought.

To enter the silent space certain sounds are used in the form of a mantra. Each person using PSM is given an individual mantra which is based on the sound that was predominating in the universe when they were born. These sounds are called seeds or *bijas* in Sanskrit. They were recorded by sages who then employed the process of Vedic mathematics to actually calculate a person's individual sound. It used to be an in-depth procedure that took many hours to calculate. Today, thanks to modern technology, a person's individual mantra can be determined in minutes.

The mantra given corresponds to the time when an individual was coming through from a non-local awareness into a localised awareness. In other words, they were coming from the gap between consciousness and matter. The mantra does not take you back to the moment of your birth, it takes you back to that point of awareness where you originally accessed universal consciousness rather than localised consciousness.

There are many different primordial sounds. The sounds of nature can have a profoundly calming effect—the rhythmic breath of ocean waves, the flowing song of a river, the whisper of the wind through the leaves, the calls of morning birds welcoming the sun. Since the beginning of humankind we have sought connection with nature by producing our own primordial sounds through chanting, drumming and singing. Cultures around the world have developed systems using rhythms and harmonic sounds to link individuals with their community, ancestral tradition and ecology. The cosmos sings a repertoire of primary vibrations over cycles of time, knowing the time and place of a person's birth allows the calculation of the appropriate mantra.

As beings with physical bodies, we too are composed of vibration. When we are living in balance with our environment our vibrations are in tune with natural rhythms — our individual song is in harmony with the cosmos. The most direct means to create this resonance is to take time each day to quiet our minds through meditation. In this state of restful alertness we can easily access our creativity and energy.

Let's move on to the significance of our dreams. It seems most researchers agree that dreams are important.
We should always remember that nature doesn't do anything for nothing. If the purpose of sleep is indeed to restore the body, we must account for the fact that during a significant portion of our sleep time this restoration isn't accomplished simply through massive rest. Instead, a positive, active process is taking place that requires significant energy — this is the process of dreaming. It makes sense then that this process is carrying out a very important physiological activity. I'll leave it to you, Leon, to explore the personal interpretations of this process.

Thanks Deepak, I think I can take over from here.

CHAPTER ONE

The
SECRETS
of SOUND SLEEP

You have a purpose,
A dream in your soul.
In fulfilling your dharma.
You will make your life whole.

DEEPAK CHOPRA

We spend about one-third of our lives in sleep. Its remarkable recuperative effects are vital to our survival. The greatest remedy for being tired is sleeping. Healthy, soothing slumber that rests muscles, nerves and our brain is nature's greatest rejuvenator. During periods of rest and sleep the body repairs itself, re-energises and prepares for renewed activity. It is as essential to life as air, water and food.

Unfortunately, in this busy, hectic—some say 'mad, mad'—world, sleep has become problematic. Certainly, dreaming isn't easy if you are one of the millions who have trouble falling asleep and staying asleep. Without quality sleep, which incorporates the phases of brainwave activity that brings our mind and body to a completely restful state, every function of our body is adversely affected. Our dreamtime is also infringed upon, often becoming little more than a confused mess.

This chapter has been designed to give you a few hints to help stop you from tossing and turning and make falling asleep a dream.

THE THIEF OF SLEEP

Social historians, studying diaries from the eighteenth and nineteenth centuries, have found that in those days people slept on average nine and a half hours a night. Today, however, our typical sleep time has dwindled to about seven and a half hours. The great thief of sleep, historians say, is the invention of synthetic light and the great array of electronic distractions (including the late-night movie) that draw back the curtain of night.

There's a simple rule for telling whether you've slept enough. If you feel rested when you wake up and don't feel tired until bedtime, providing that it is not too late, you have probably had sufficient sleep.

My research indicates that when asked, most people quote sleeping eight to eight and a half hours a night, although between seven and seven and a half hours is perhaps a more exact estimate. Others can get away with sleeping only five and a half to six and a half hours a night, while others sleep up to ten hours. There's even the select few who sleep less than five and a half hours a night. Generally, most people are satisfied with seven to nine hours sleep.

Cheating on sleep is a stressful condition. Your body will

adjust to the odd night of short sleep, say one or two hours less than what you felt you needed, but if you miss more than two hours a night, or miss necessary sleep consistently, physical, emotional and spiritual symptoms may develop.

One-third of all people in the Western world complain of fatigue. The figure is closer to half the population when surveying only city dwellers. One of the major factors, without doubt, is that we try to do too much in our lives. Many of us want to achieve more and often it's a case of rush, rush, rush. We work hard to pay our mortgages, keep our businesses afloat, pay off our holidays or our kids' school fees. As a consequence, we spend our free time rushing around trying to make the most of the little time we have.

The net result is less sleep and rest than we really need. When this becomes a consistent pattern in our lives, our bodies lose the ability to recharge and chronic fatigue sets in. The irony about all of this is that if we want to achieve more, we should really sleep and rest more. Only then will our bodies and minds be in top shape to take on the tasks we set ourselves.

Researchers say sleep deprivation can heighten the risk of under achievement at work or school, increase the risk of being in an accident on the road, at work or in the home, and increase the chances of being involved in a stressful argument. If you consider it for a moment, we actually save time by our ability to think clearly after a good night's sleep. Decisions are made easier and tasks can be prioritised correctly.

Sound sleep is more than just closing your eyes. The late Dr David Phillips—philosopher, health researcher, numerologist and author of the bestselling book *Discovering the Inner Self*—believed insufficient restful sleep plagues most people at some time in their lives. He once said to me, restlessness induces emotionally-charged dreams that can further contribute to the feeling of continued tiredness, and that no-one should underestimate the importance of regular, restful sleep.

THE ART OF NAPPING

Our bodies are naturally inclined to feel a little sleepy in the early to middle hours of the afternoon. This is particularly so if we eat a large meal at lunchtime. Afternoon napping — 15 to 30 minutes — is a wonderful way to restore a flagging body. Afternoon naps, or power naps as they are referred to in some circles, tend to be rich in the most restful phase of sleep, making them an effective tool for catching up on lost slumber. A short nap in the afternoon can often leave you more rested than the same amount of time tacked on to your morning sleep.

Napping isn't always feasible. But try to grab a catnap whenever you can, even if only on weekends. When you nap it is possible to feel groggy for five to 15 minutes afterwards. This is normal and part of a phenomenon known as sleep inertia. Sleep inertia occurs after both daytime and night-time sleep; the deeper the sleep, the more pronounced the effects. Most researchers agree with what nappers already know — that the temporary inconvenience of sleep inertia is more than made up for by improved alertness and a buoyant mood later in the day.

Afternoon naps are also a great avenue for going into a dream state — whether it be a true dream or a creative daydream in which you can visualise positive things for your life. The art of daydreaming is covered in Chapter Five.

SSSHHH! I'M TRYING TO GET TO SLEEP ...

Here are some tips for sound sleep:

Still the mind

Take time out to let your body slow down before you retire. Read a spiritually uplifting book or listen to some soft music. Music is wonderful relaxation therapy and uplifting to the spirit. Talk quietly with a loved one or a companion.

Read

Reading can be a very soothing activity which focuses the mind. Obviously choosing material that brings peace and relaxation to your thoughts is much more appropriate than reading a spy thriller or horror story. A 'soft' novel can take your thoughts away from the day's agenda — worry and concern being one of the most encroaching factors on reaching a sleep state. Sometimes reading a manual, especially the one that comes with your video, can bring faster results because your mind becomes tired with facts and figures and decides to shut down.

Make sure you have a decent reading lamp which you can switch on and off near your bed. There is no point having to get up to turn the light off when you are about to drop off to sleep.

Establish a sleep pattern

The body likes to work to a routine. Establish a sleep pattern and try to stick roughly to it. In other words, go to bed and get up around the same time each day, although don't be frightened to catch a few extra winks if you can afford the time. The idea is not to go to bed at 9 p.m. three nights of the week and 3 a.m. four nights of the week.

Avoid sleeping pills

Sleeping pills can be dangerous to your health and one would need to be under strict medical direction to continue taking them over a long period. Because of the composition and the effect of a sleeping pill, the dream process is drastically altered. Look for natural ways to better sleep if you feel you need an aid, but use them for only a short period. There are numerous herbs, homoeopathic mixtures and/or nutritional supplement blends which can help the body to better sleep, but they shouldn't be relied upon long-term.

Dreaming is the oldest natural therapy. The more natural we can keep the dream state the greater the opportunity for the healing processes to occur.

Go easy on liquids

If you have trouble getting back to sleep after midnight trips to the bathroom, limit your liquid intake before bedtime. Although a cocktail or two may help you fall asleep, alcohol can also wake you in the middle of the night or early the next morning. Bear in mind that some of the world's worst sleepers and dreamers are heavy drinkers. As for that cup of coffee after dinner, skip it if you notice it gives you a boost. In fact, coffee taken within seven hours of bedtime can interfere with sleep.

No à la carte dreaming

Don't eat just before you go to bed. This is an oft forgotten piece of advice. It is not wise to go to bed on a full stomach as the body cannot easily digest food that has been eaten just before bedtime. Many people are kept awake by the lively squeaks and rumbles resounding from their tummies after a heavy meal—it's not exactly a relaxating sonata! It can invariably bring about a restless and often exhausting night's sleep, and sometimes a few bad dreams, too.

If you are hungry, have a small, light meal. A piece of fruit or a sandwich perhaps. Better still, a camomile herb tea which can help put you to sleep. Stay away from regular tea and coffee at all costs. Camomile is the herb that put Peter Rabbit to sleep, and it tops the list of natural sleep inducers.

If you don't have any food sensitivities, allergies or mood and energy fluctuations, a cup of hot chocolate can also be a good snooze inducer. Warm milk or soy milk is good on occasions. Never boil milk, only warm it as boiling it will destroy vital enzymes, thereby making it difficult to digest.

Take a warm shower or bath

This can sometimes loosen tense muscles and help you to relax. It can also be a meditative action where you make a decision to wash away the day's cares, leaving them alone until you wake.

Smell yourself to sleep

A great way to slip into never-never land quickly is to stimulate your sense of smell, in conjunction with any of the above suggestions. Vaporisers (or oil burners) are readily available from most holistic retailers. My good friends, Karen Downes and Judith White, authors of *Aromatherapy for Scentual Awareness* and regarded by many as two of the most respected aromatherapists in the world, recommended to me a blend of equal parts of marjoram, orange and lavender for the following reasons: marjoram is the most sedating, orange is uplifting and relaxing, and lavender is soothing and calming. Burning the oils in a vaporiser is one of my favourite methods of inducing sleep. Not only does the fragrance assist me in drifting away, the soft flickering of the light created by the candle in the vaporiser seems to put me into a sleep rhythm because it's so natural, gentle and flowing.

For those who are not familiar with this safe, therapeutic practice, aromatherapy is the use of pure essential oils which have been derived from plants. It has been used to enhance healing, relaxation, meditation and prayer for thousands of years. The ancient Egyptians and Greeks used plant oils such as frankincense and myrrh for adornment and worship, Arabic medicine in medieval times consisted of recipes using herbs, flowers and spices to cure illness, and incense has been burned by many cultures to connect with God. Today, a resurgence of this powerful therapy is being used to bring about wellbeing with the support of scientific validation. Aromatherapy is a way for people to stay in touch with nature and receive its wonderful benefits through the sense of smell.

Wayne Dyer

This dream may have taken place in Egypt because the most prominent feature in this dream was a pyramid. As I walked towards the pyramid, I noticed the huge stones were actually humans. I looked up into their faces and recognised my children. I then remember climbing up to become part of this 'human' pyramid.

Karen and Judith have conducted experiments and research in relation to aromatherapy and dream recall. Their research shows that dreams can be remembered with increased clarity by triggering the memory through the sense of smell. The essential oil blend you choose to help you drift off to sleep can be used again the following morning when you wish to interpret your dreams. The fragrance invokes a memory in the same way hot apple pie and icecream may remind you of your grandmother's home or the oil on an old rag of your father's garage. Judith and Karen recommend preparing an extra portion of the evening blend to ensure that the fragrance is exactly the same when used the following morning.

For a better night's sleep, Karen and Judith recommend placing these oils in your vaporiser (place water in the bowl before adding the drops):

Orange	(four drops)
Marjoram	(two drops)
Lavender	(four drops)

For connecting to your higher self they recommend:

Orange	(four drops)
Clary Sage	(two drops)
Frankincense	(three drops)

For connecting to your life's direction they recommend:

Clary Sage	(three drops)
Myrrh	(two drops)
Bergamot	(four drops)

Get physical

Improve your sex life. An exchange of bodily energy with a partner has long been renowned as an effective sleep inducer. If you don't have a regular partner why not create a dream lover?

Healthy sex is an excellent bed companion for sleep. The chemicals released through orgasm and physical sexual activity actually send signals to the brain for it to switch off once intercourse has been completed. Neurotransmitters are also stimulated which brings the pleasant feelings of wellbeing and contentment—the perfect recipe for sound sleep.

For those who are alone, whether it be through travel, being single, or separated from one's partner, sex can still be a sleep inducer. Although masturbation has been condemned for thousands of years, as we head towards the next millennium the cultural taboos associated with it are slowly disappearing. This is a huge subject and I realise that the guilt attached to masturbation is still a big issue, but I do believe we can be mature enough to understand that not everybody has a partner to share their sexual experiences and needs with.

According to Betty Dodson, PhD, author of *Sex for One*, masturbation provides sexual satisfaction for people without partners. She says, 'It is relaxing and helps induce sleep ... it is also certainly a basic form of safe sex.'

Studies have also proven that touch is a therapeutic method for bringing relaxation and releasing tension. The sensation of touch is deeply connected to the emotional centre (or limbic system) within our brain. Children and babies who are deprived of touch can be greatly affected, sometimes developing dysfunctional behaviour patterns as adults. Alternatively, adults, who generally suffer from sleep problems more readily than children, can also be disadvantaged by the lack of affection and physical caring associated with touch. The sharing of affection and the physical sensation of care through the touch of an intimate partner is extremely beneficial for easing anxiety and coaxing a state of peace, security and tranquillity.

Make a bed worth lying in

Invest in a good, comfortable bed. Don't skimp on bed quality or size. Similarly, find a pillow you like and take it with you when you are sleeping out of your home, if it's convenient.

If you live in a cold climate, take a hot water bottle to bed and place it near your feet. Hot water bottles are a much healthier alternative to electric blankets, which can affect sensitive individuals and often leave them feeling drained of energy.

Anti-sleep theory

If all else fails, force yourself to stay awake by trying to convince your mind that you really don't want to sleep and you want to be active by reading or completing some task. Some reverse psychological trickery causes your mind to say, 'Hey, I'm tired, let's sleep.'

David Suzuki

One of my most vivid dreams was one where I was flying over a vast landscape of forests, trees, lakes and mountains. I recall a feeling of being able to control and observe the dream at will.

Make optimism your nightcap

Before you go to bed dismiss negative emotions. Focus on thoughts that are uplifting and pleasing. Mentally place yourself in a scene that is supportive and full of choices. The old maxim 'Don't let the sun go down on your wrath' is still as valid today as when it was written.

Get a friend to massage your feet

Foot massage is a wonderful relaxant. It is believed by those practicing Oriental medicine and reflexology that the organs in the body are connected by 'meridians' to specific areas of the foot. Therefore, massaging the feet can have a healing and relaxing effect on the entire body. *In Aromatherapy for Lovers and Dreamers*, a book I co-authored with Judith White and Karen Downes, an aromatherapy foot massage is suggested that soothes tired and aching feet, bringing relaxation to the whole body. The following essential oil blend is especially good for making feet sweet:

Peppermint	(one drop)
Basil	(two drops)
Bergamot	(two drops)

Add these oil drops to 10 mls of base massage oil such as wheatgerm, apricot, avocado or sesame oil. Now smoothe the blend over your companion's feet and gently begin to massage them one at a time using your intuition to guide your technique.

If your companion won't do your feet choose another part of your anatomy, but use the sweet feet blend only on the feet!

The big rewind

A method you may like to try to help you fall asleep is to review your day backwards. Rudolph Steiner's method of running through your actions backwards was intended to make you a spectator to your day.

Trevor Ravenscroft, one of the finest metaphysicians I have known, suggested the technique could be used for effective sleep inducement. Imagine your day as if you were watching a movie running in reverse. Relax and begin to rewind in your mind every action starting with your head on the pillow. In other words, see yourself rising from your bed, walking backwards, turning on the light, walking into the bathroom, toothpaste going back into the tube, the cup being placed into the cupboard, the cupboard being closed, you yawning, back into the living room, etc. This process is so unusual for the mind that it can't wait to shut down. Try it. It works.

The methods I've discussed are inappropriate in extreme cases of insomnia but are very useful in ensuring that the stage is set to dream the interpretable dream.

CHAPTER TWO

I (Also) HAD a DREAM

Everything I see has roots in the unseen world
Nature reflects my moods
The body and mind may sleep
I am always awake.

DEEPAK CHOPRA

It seems highly likely that the experience we call dreaming could be the bridge between our physical and spiritual life — the ethereal link between the conscious and the unconscious. Perhaps, if we acknowledge our dreams, we can cross this bridge into an infinite world of balance, creativity and abundance — just by batting an eyelid.

How we learn from dreams — and utilise the information obtained from these mental images — has been the basis of much study by some of the world's greatest philosophers, researchers and presenters of information in the field of personal growth. Plato, Aristotle, Descartes, Freud and Jung all postulated that dreams are a window to understanding the human mind and, indeed, closely related to our everyday lives.

They are not simply random, senseless images caused by over-active brain signals.

I assume you are fascinated, intrigued or mystified—perhaps all three—by your dreams. The fact that you even picked up this book indicates an interest. You may already have some intuitive belief that dreams can tell you something about yourself, and that they can bring you face to face with a galaxy of hidden talents and potentialities that are quietly resting in the recesses of your mind.

I Must Be Dreaming has been written to demonstrate the ability you have to develop more skills to interpret your own dreams successfully and show you how to expand upon them. In doing so, I have not concentrated on the meaning of particular symbols you encounter while dreaming but on sharpening your knowledge of how the images which parade through your mind at night may fit into your life.

We can look beyond the surface of our dreams to uncover the hidden treasures lying deep within our subconscious. There is an unlimited potential of spiritual wealth and beauty lying underneath the daily conscious reality of life we experience. By understanding the nature of our dreams, we can further explore the realms of intuition and discover the essence of who we are with greater clarity and insight.

I encourage you to use this book as a guiding hand in the same fashion as you would use a tourist guidebook if you were about to visit foreign shores for the first time. In such a book the authors may detail the points of interest and how to go about finding them, but ultimately, the adventure is all yours.

TONIGHT'S THE NIGHT

Scientists have proven that everyone dreams, even people who are blind. Although it is possible to have as few as three or as many as nine dreams a night, generally you have around four to five dreams during eight hours of shut-eye. In fact, you spend approximately twenty per cent of your total sleep time dreaming, which calculates to an hour and a half a night, or three episodes of *The Simpsons*.

The most basic tenet for sleep is to recharge our physical body, address unresolved emotional issues and to file valuable information we regularly collect into our memory databanks. In recent years, knowledge has also been accumulating that indicates the ego and the subconscious mind encounter some really great adventures together during sleep which are vital for the expansion of our consciousness. That is, dreams allow us to enter a playground of unlimited possibilities.

Every night as we sleep, we enter into another level of awareness—another form of existence where people, places and other things we may or may not recognise in our waking reality appear. We can be far away in another country, making love to the partner of our 'dreams', or even switching from one 'life' or 'movie script' to another. We can visit people and see them at different ages, alter their size and appearance and even become another entity ourselves. During our dreams we ignore the usual restraints of time and space so that we experience the cryptic world of our psyche without the barriers of our waking life such as our social conditioning and our defence mechanisms. Dreams are not discriminating, they lay everything out before us, whether we like it or not.

For those of us who have good dream recall, or who work on remembering their dreams and developing this ability, dreamtime can be an exciting, weird and wonderful part of our existence. How often have you heard someone say, 'I had the strangest dream last night?' And then go into great detail about the flying toothbrush or whatever captured their imagination while asleep. Quite often, when retelling their dreams, they gain insight and enlightenment as to what significance the dream had upon their life.

On the surface, dreams seem to be an entire world of invention, fiction and imagination. But are they? Underneath our layers of consciousness, dreams play a much more phenomenal role than we often give credence for. In dreams we see people, events and places that we don't recall or remember in our ordinary waking state; some people even get 'hunches' from dreams, such as new directions in a business deal, receiving images of their perfect partner or selecting lottery numbers. A prominent doctor once told me that he actually asked his dream life to predict the fall of the ball on the roulette wheel while he was on a holiday. He dreamed a specific number and the following evening when he played the game, the predicted number came up! This event shows the power of our subconscious, but it can be illusory. When I asked my dream life for the numbers it replied, 'Not unless I get 50 per cent of the takings!'

If you care to research it, you can actually find documented evidence that suggests dreams can foretell the future. For example, Abraham Lincoln is said to have had a dream revealing his own assassination. He stated that in this dream, on hearing people sobbing, he wandered downstairs to see what was happening. When he reached the East Room, he saw a coffin and a corpse whose face was covered. He asked a soldier who it was and the soldier replied: '[It's] the President.' Lincoln was killed by an assassin.

Recurring dreams, which feature the same characters, can occur frequently in the land of nod, and serialised dreams that begin one night and continue into another are also experienced ... imagine having your own version of the *X Files* where Mulder discovers the only truth out there is that he has the hots for Scully!

Many people report they have been woken by something dramatic that happened in their dreams, whether it be someone speaking, a loud noise, falling down a hole or off a cliff (a common experience) and when they have been brought to orgasm! This latter phenomenon is known as nocturnal emission, also common, but more pleasurable than falling off a cliff. Then there are the dreams, or nightmares, where a tragic or stressful event may have taken place in waking life and is repeated during sleep—scientific research has claimed this is an important part of the healing process.

Why is all this so? Stop and think about it for a minute. Allow your mind to let go of all the rationales which prevent you from seeing dreams in a judgement-free environment. Is it possible that all of these images we know as dreams represent some form of mental classification of all our experiences? Are dreams processing the information we have taken in at various levels of consciousness?

Just imagine, you are storing all of your experiences in a library, and you need to flick through the index occasionally to find out where this or that book belongs. Your thought processes skip from image to image as you look at the index cards. It is quite likely that you would begin to daydream about past events just by looking at these index cards and recalling past experiences. You may also fantasise about things you would like to have happened in your life. Like the library, our subconscious is a storehouse of information that our soul browses nightly, searching to make meaning of all our daily encounters.

We know for certain that, while the body rests, much mental activity takes place. A person can, during sleep, solve intricate problems, the answers to which have eluded them during the day. We can also tell the time and wake at any hour decided upon, provided our body is functioning of its own accord and without stimulants or relaxants.

All these factors point to a very intelligent, in-built system. Although we have not yet realised the full potential of our dreamings, one thing can be sure, dreams expand our consciousness.

NIGHTMARES FOR DAYSTALLIONS

To explain the nightmare let's consider the natural balance and harmony of the human body. When we are in good health we rarely have sleep interrupted by disturbing dreams, provided there is no interference from alcohol or drugs, and food is being digested correctly in the body and. eaten well before bedtime. When the body is thrown out of balance, through drugs, stress, work, interpersonal strain, supplements or whatever, your dreams will reflect your altered chemical, physical or mental state.

Who hasn't had a nightmare after suffering from a feverish condition such as a bad flu? Who hasn't slept and dreamt fitfully during a period of great stress in their life? Remember always that the dream state is as delicately balanced as the body's metabolism. I read an article in a magazine recently that suggested nightmares are more likely to occur when we feel our boundaries are thin; that is, when we feel vulnerable and have low self-esteem. But nightmares are not necessarily a negative experience. Nightmares give us the opportunity to release our fears and our frustrations in the dream state; thus they allow us to get some of our most negative experiences out in the open where we can deal with them.

DREAM SPEAK

Dreaming is an important part of our total existence. Many of us in the modern world have lost touch with the symbolic language that is dream speech. I believe we can reawaken this ability to interpret our dreams—we are all experts on what the dream means, they are our very own creations.

We already have the ability to understand the messages our dreams are revealing. When we ignore our dreams and thought processes, we may be turning our back on a profound portion of our individuality. I believe that the gift of imagination should be seen as breath to the psyche in the same way as oxygen is to the body. In this way, dreams are an essential part of life.

I've often asked myself, how much can I expect to learn from my dreams from a mystical and scientific point of view? Both ancient and modern philosophers have spoken about the heightened capacity for insight during sleep. The author Synesius of Cyrene (370-413), wrote, 'We do not sleep merely to live, but to learn to live well.' Sigmund Freud noted, 'Sleep offers itself to all: it is an oracle always ready to be our infallible and silent counsellor.'

From a scientific perspective, there is evidence to suggest dreams are crucial samples of our emotional, psychological and spiritual states—just as the chemical components in a sample of blood are of great diagnostic importance to your doctor when studying your health and the condition of your body.

I could load you down with an avalanche of scientific facts, but I've no intention of doing that in this book. I'm sure some are already aware of Sigmund Freud's postulations of dreams being a revelation of deep, hidden desires, and it does seem likely that some of our dreams are wish fulfilments. Although I wouldn't go so far as to say that every dream symbol has sexual connotations. Personally I feel more comfortable with Carl Jung's work—it seems a little less rigid. He said, 'Dreams may give expressions to ineluctable truths, to philosophical pronouncements, illusions, wild fantasies ... and heaven knows what besides.' Sleep can be an amazing place.

Consider the thoughts of Dr Ann Faraday, who has given much insight into the significance of dreams:

In forming a bridge between body, mind and spirit, it is possible that dreams may be used as a springboard from which a human can leap to new realms of experience lying outside their normal state of consciousness and enlarge their own vision, not only of himself, but also of the universe in which he lives.

Jane Fleming

I was strolling through a dark forest when I came across the path of a huge grizzly bear. The bear started to chase me. After running a little way I noticed an owl stick its head up from a burrow in the ground. I jumped into the burrow. I remember feeling content and safe in the owl's presence.

CHAPTER THREE

To DREAM the INTERPRETABLE DREAM

Privileged children of the cosmos
Nothing is separate from you
Deep inside the fabric of matter and energy
There are gods and goddesses in embryo waiting to be born.

DEEPAK CHOPRA

D reams are described by some as the mysterious language of the night, by others as the information our brain needs to create memory. I think they are both. Throughout the ages, men and women of all cultures have accepted that dreams could perhaps foretell the future or reveal long-forgotten images of the past. It is believed by many that our experiences during sleep time can provide us with enlightening information that can assist us to achieve the highest possible level of personal development.

Most of us who have come as far as buying a book on dreams realise that our dreams certainly contain creative inspiration. To unlock these natural reservoirs of insight we need to be able to interpret our dreams in our own individual way and to act upon this information. Each and every one of us is psychic. We all experience different levels of this ability which is determined in part by our active exercise to develop this power. The human psychic abilities are no different to their physical counterparts. If you're willing to race off to the gymnasium each day and work on your stomach muscles, you are going to end up with a very flat and strong abdominal region. In the same fashion, if you're willing to work on the intuitive aspect of your mind, you will quickly develop the ability to perceive the lessons and messages that your dream state is transmitting. How this information comes to you is really not important to understand at this point. What is important, is to realise that you have psychic abilities and that you can develop them to whatever level you desire. The key is intuition. How many times have you said to yourself, 'I should have trusted my first instincts?' How many times has your gut feeling told you that someone was trustworthy even though you had no direct experience to go on—quite the opposite; others had told you that the individual could not be trusted but you went with your gut feelings and everything turned out okay? Intuition has been a part of our psyche since the beginning of time. Every indigenous culture has relied upon and still holds sacred this spiritual gift, honouring it as part of their ancestor's lore. Now that we are in the middle of a highly technical age, science has replaced intuition. But the pendulum is beginning to swing the other way, and even the most academic amongst us are acknowledging that not everything can be so black and white, there are many grey areas, too. It's in these areas that intuition can be found like a beacon on a cold, wind-swept night.

There are countless ways to delve into the meaning of your dreams but without completely trusting your intuition it's like trying to fill the Grand Canyon with a teaspoon. Following are five easy ways to fine-tune your intuition that I have found to be very beneficial:

1. Read Agatha Christie books and try to work out 'who done it?' before you get to the last page.

2. Never pick up a phone that rings without trying to sense who is on the line.

3. Find something you have lost without asking anyone for assistance.

4. As often as possible get to as many locations as you can without asking for directions.

5. Go with your gut feelings.

I believe one should relax and have fun with dream interpretation and not see every dream as a prophetic signpost or omen. Dream interpretation is speculation on what dreams mean. As you develop your dream analysis capabilities you will be able to distinguish between what is memory manufactured — what is basically last night's peperoni pizza while watching the *Return of the Living Dead* — and what is a significant message from your subconscious. It's important not to become obsessed by trying to find deep meaning within every interpretation. Become accustomed to intuitively chiselling out those ones you really believe have a message while discarding the rest.

Quite simply, don't take the interpretation too seriously. Feel relaxed about it. Enjoy the journey to self discovery. Once you become proficient in analysing your dreams, you may be tempted to interpret the dreams of others. Assist them, but don't pass judgement. Let them interpret their own dreams according to their individuality. Encourage them to look within. If someone wants to understand their dreams, they are seeking a better understanding of themselves.

Chapter Four discusses broad archetypal meanings which may assist you with interpreting the key elements in your dreams. Space has also been left in this section for you to list your own interpretations of symbols in order to create your own dreamer's guide. When you are analysing a dream, consider what it could mean to you, then go to your dreamer's guide and decide if there is a relevant message in the dream.

From time to time it is important to review and update your recognition of different symbols because as we change and grow, symbols will acquire other meanings. I personally prefer the concept that the meaning of symbols defined in dream dictionaries is only a basic guide. Many people use the term 'dream dictionary' but a dictionary implies this is the only language of a specific culture and is limited in its interpretation of what each symbol means. I believe they should be called 'dreamer's guides' because it is virtually impossible for only one meaning of a symbol to be accepted when we are all individuals. For example, you dream that you are under a tree and a maiden hands you an apple, and you ask yourself what the image means. If you are a greengrocer then you might assume it would imply abundance because that is how you earn your living. But what if you are a fruit picker? It may indicate hard work ahead. If you are a person who is very religious it may be a warning for you to be wary because forbidden fruits are going to be handed to you. If you are a teacher, acknowledgement is a closely associated interpretation. Finally, if you've just discovered the wonderful world of computers, the dream may mean you are going to get a job at the Apple Macintosh headquarters! The interpretation is completely subjective. What a dreamer's guide should be is a prompt to stimulate your thinking. Look at your background, your profession and the space that you are in now and write down the meaning of the word apple. I guarantee in 12 months time whatever you wrote down will be altered in some way because you have progressed to a different space.

THE MORNING AFTER

Upon waking there is sometimes only a light mist of a memory. Elusive fragments of dreams quickly disappear and the hazy clouds clear until you realise you are here, now, awake. Occasionally, a dream is so vivid you almost feel you could walk easily back into it. You may immediately launch into a full-scale summary of what went on in your dream to your partner beside you, or to a friend or family member on the telephone. Very often these vivid dreams will tug at your consciousness and you wonder what they mean for your life today, or tomorrow.

There are many methods that you can use to interpret your dreams, but before you can do that you must be able to recall them. When I wake up—before I empty out the bladder and put on the kettle—I focus on the main symbols, feelings and events of the dream, and from there begin to work out their meaning. If you don't feel like working on it immediately, write the dream symbols in a dream journal and return to it later. Researchers say we have a ten minute window of opportunity to work with, before the mists set in and the symbols begin to fade. If you don't remember many of your dreams, here are five possible reasons why:

1. You didn't feel they were worth remembering.
2. You were hanging out with your spirit guides the night before—Bacardi and Johnnie Walker.
3. You were in a very deep sleep.
4. You were woken up suddenly and instantly distracted.
5. You're an insomniac and don't know it.

Now, here are five suggestions on how to remember your dreams.

1. Wake up naturally (and then get dressed!).
2. Keep a dream journal.
3. Hold your dream life in high regard.
4. Cultivate a dream lover.
5. Continually enjoy waking up to yourself.

Now that you know the best ways to remember your dreams and the reasons why you don't, you can begin to look at the many methods of interpretation. Remember, the method by which you interpret your dream is less important than the meaning you personally derive from it. You may look at each dream as a separate and new revelation, or view your dreams over time as a collective whole.

Jimmy Barnes

I have a recurring dream where I'm in a milkbar or coffee shop and outside the shop is this beam of pure white light. As I get up to walk towards it, someone or something taps me on the shoulder. I get distracted and the light disappears.

Following, are some traditionally used methods of dream interpretation which can be very effective. Have fun, loosen up and treat it as if you're about to embark on an overseas trip full of adventure and enlightenment. It's not necessary to look at it as a heroic quest in search of your 'Holy Grail' and the meaning of life. Enlightenment and personal development come when you least expect them, and when you are not worrying about them.

Once you've decided that it would be useful to understand the meaning behind the symbols you saw in a dream, the next step is to invest in a decent-sized diary and use it as a dream journal. From the outset, don't make it a laborious task where you have to sit down for hours writing about your experiences the night before. Simply jot down short sentences that help to jog your memory about the circumstances of a particular symbol. Sometimes just writing down the symbol is enough. For example, if you dreamt you were sitting in a brand new car driving to work and a large, red-headed dog bit your tyres and you were stranded, it's enough to write: me, car, red-headed dog, deflated, lack of mobility — that's five quick prompts that take no time to enter yet truly cover the situation. It's more than enough to bring the symbology and feeling behind the dream out of the ether and into the physical. Don't bog yourself down with a long-winded essay each time you write down a dream, unless you are the type of individual that has the time and the inclination to do so and it actually gives you pleasure. For the individual who is not inclined to write things down and prefers audio communication, then a tape recorder is simple yet very effective. Purchase a box of tapes that are solely dedicated to your audio dream journal, and ensure that you never run out of tape — there's nothing worse than trying to remember a dream while stressed out because everything is not at your fingertips.

USING YOUR DREAM GUIDE

Begin by going back and remembering any dream symbols that are still vivid in your mind. Under the Dreamer's Guide on page 83 write down your interpretation to the symbols mentioned. 'Apple' was my first word. I wrote the following for this symbol: good health; forbidden fruit (a female handed me an apple in the dream); consistency in the fact that there is a never-ending supply throughout the year. In this way you build up a dream guide that is totally, absolutely and definitely unique to yourself. This guide need never have an ending and should be expanded at regular intervals as new icons and symbols appear and become noteworthy.

In Chapter Four I have also included a number of interesting perceptions about different symbols. They may amuse you or enlighten you, but remember they are only a guide.

DON'T FORGET DREAM MOTIFS

A dream motif is a theme, an action, or a situation that recurs during your dream state. A motif, by definition, is a distinctive idea, so look for the many exceptional situations that are experienced while dreaming—the most common is flying, closely followed by falling, climbing, running and making love. To understand your dream more completely, try to acknowledge as many motifs as possible. You need to identify motifs because it's not only the symbol but the setting of the dream that is important. If you dreamt that you were picking pineapples in the middle of Alaska during a snowstorm it would carry a different meaning than if you dreamt you were picking pineapples in the middle of summer in northern Queensland. The first description indicates that your tasks and ideals are not in harmony. If you are in tune with your life and what is happening around you, naturally you are going to pick the pineapples in the Queensland environment as opposed to the Alaskan environment.

Motifs can also help you tune into your emotions. For example, you may be having dreams about all sorts of activities where falling is always a component. You may be writing a letter and you fall, or playing golf or tennis and again falling at some point during the dream. You need to consider the motif of falling and ask yourself why you feel unsupported in everything you do. Falling represents (from an archetypal perspective) a feeling that you don't have anything solid underneath you and are not being supported. By being made fully aware of this emotion you can easily begin to sift through your life and address any problems or weaknesses you may not have noticed prior to the subconscious signals.

DEVELOP AN UNDERSTANDING OF YOUR DREAMS

The most obvious thing to do would be to go out and buy books on the subject of dreams, attend seminars or perhaps listen to tapes. These can be very useful. However, be very selective and endeavour to keep these particular activities to a minimum.

If your dream was a song, and the symbols and motifs were the notes, the best plan in learning to play the song would be to firstly learn where the notes are on your instrument. You can then put them together in your individual style and listen to your own interpretation. It's quite simple — learn where the notes are and play your own tune. The idea is to go beyond relying on someone else for your interpretations — play it by ear.

One path to understanding and interpreting dreams is to start within your own family circle. Go to the oldest members of the family and speak to them about dreams. They are living connections with your ancestors and will be able to give you insights around the beliefs and perceptions you are dealing with.

Mediterranean peoples have a different attitude towards life to, let's say, people from Asian backgrounds. So, if you come from a Mediterranean background and you dream that someone is serving you a meal of only boiled rice, you could quite rightly conclude that this individual is offering you a meagre form of survival or very mediocre possibilities in life. However, if you are of Asian background, the opposite would be true, as rice is the basis of all meals, and therefore would have a different connotation. Whoever was supplying you with this bowl of rice may be offering you something that is the very essence of your survival. So it's important to interpret events within your cultural background.

Another suggestion is to regularly read articles and books, and go to the movies and watch videos. The idea here is to see how someone else's thoughts are demonstrated through their own perceptions. By broadening your outlook of life, you will automatically expand your ability to create new realities for yourself. A line in a movie that is heard and forgotten by everyone else in the theatre, may spark insights for you because it's the missing piece of a dream jigsaw that you were trying to put together. A great example that was most profound to me occurred when I was watching a detective series called *A Touch of Frost*. A young constable alluded to Inspector Frost that he was the most disorganised, unstructured, non-conservative person on the Force, and yet was amazed how Frost was able to solve the mystery. Frost replied to the constable that he should never be concerned about walking out of step with others because by doing this you touch ground that no-one else touches. In that one second I gained illuminating information. I realised that when you go against the grain you explore territory no-one else walks upon and you can come up with new concepts, new realisations, new methods of doing things, even though it can feel awkward or lonely. It's a prime example of when you least expect it, you can be watching some inconsequential movie or television program for entertainment and out of the blue a cosmic revelation can 'pow' you right between your eyes. I suggest you look for those little one-liners during your dreams, or while at the flicks. It can add incredible meaning to your life.

LISTEN TO YOUR DREAM FEELING

Sometimes upon awakening one can feel exactly the same way as after a hard day's work. There is not much difference between coming home, sitting down and feeling exhausted after a day of running around, or waking up and feeling exhausted after a heavy night's dreaming. There are occasions when we feel satisfaction after a day's work; refreshed, invigorated, more abundant and wiser. These same emotions can also be felt upon awakening after a dream.

On waking, reflect on your feelings and emotions and bring into focus the journey that has brought you to the point of this particular experience; ask yourself what has transpired to make you feel that way. Denise Linn wrote in *Pocketful of Dreams*,

Find the feeling or emotion that you had as a result of your dream. Now look back over your life and remember the last time you had that feeling. Recall the situation which evoked that similar emotion. Most often it is either that particular situation or the issues underlying that situation that have evoked your dream. This can be a real clue to assist you in finding the significance of your dream.

While you are awake and working, a co-worker could irritate you and cause you to experience anger for the rest of the afternoon. If you dream the same situation, the same emotion can be experienced and you'll awake feeling angry. Feelings are very important when it comes to understanding the message contained in a dream. By remembering the feeling and emotion, as well as the symbol, your understanding becomes even deeper and more productive.

TALK WITH A SAGE

The dictionary meaning of the word 'sage' is an individual who is wise and prudent. Look around and observe the individuals who you believe have these qualities. Age, background or profession should have no bearing. Tradespeople can provide completely different perceptions to academics because they work with their hands so they usually have different views on life to people who work with their minds. So when you decide to talk to a sage don't hold any judgements about profession, age or gender. The only criteria should be that you respect the person as an individual.

Once you've decided to sit down with a sage, endeavour to have a free-flowing conversation about perspectives on life. Do more listening than talking. It's not necessary to divulge the fact that you are working on methods that will assist you to interpret your dreams. I have found that you pick up more information that assists in the interpretation of your dreams in general conversation, and in sharing feelings.

DRAW YOUR DREAMS

After a very vivid, emotional or thought-provoking dream, I have found it useful to try and recreate a physical impression of the most important scene. For the artists among us, it's quite easy to draw the scene and illustrate it in detail. If that's not appropriate for you, then try the following: start with a scene that you've cut out of a magazine or newspaper that reminds you of the background in the dream. Then search through every newspaper and magazine in your possession and cut out images that relate to the dream scene you want to reconstruct. Place these images on the background scene and begin to recreate your dream scene. The key to this is not to rush. Put together as much as you can with the resources available. As you come across other photographs or images that fit, add them to the scene until you feel it's complete. At this point, meditate and ponder on the relevance this scene has on your life at this time.

While this process is taking place, I strongly recommend that you keep it as private as you can and avoid explaining what

Louise Hay

My most memorable dreams always take place in my garden. Everything seems to grow bigger, brighter and more fragrant each time I return.

you're doing. Also avoid unsolicited comments or directions from people around you. The picture you are creating is personal and should go in a direction that is only governed by your intuition with no outside influences. Once you have completed your image, then show it to whomever you like. It's like going on a long journey, following the directions as your heart dictates.

BECOMING THE SYMBOL

No dreamer's guide would be complete without recommending the work of world-renowned dream interpreter Fritz Perls. His technique of 'becoming' the symbol can be one of the most useful tools in dream analysis. If someone says, 'I dreamt I was walking down a tunnel,' the first thing you do is bring it into the present tense and close your eyes and say, 'I am walking down a tunnel now.'

If you recount a dream in past tense, then you're remembering it with the use of your conscious mind. But when you say, 'I am walking down a tunnel' you are in the present tense of the dream and you therefore have a tendency to recover the same kind of alpha brainwave patterns that you had while you were having the dream.

Fritz suggests that you adopt the significant symbols as part of your identity during the interpretation. For instance, slowly, in your mind, become the tunnel. Begin to think what it feels like being that tunnel ... 'I am walking down a tunnel, I am the tunnel, I am unseen, I am something through which things pass on their way to their destiny. I just stay here, unseen, and then people emerge from me, they do so without realising that I made the journey possible.'

This kind of dream is typical of people who feel that they are displaced, that nobody identifies their talents, and that others just pass by and get the accolades. Creative individuals, feeling they've got potential, often uncover this theme. Because you become the symbol in the dream, you can find out exactly what's going on. At the same time you can detach yourself sufficiently from the situation to get a different perspective about the message in your dream. In that moment, when the message of the dream is clear, it could be that you have resolved the situation.

We usually dream about situations that are unresolved. Once we overcome the problem or create an answer, in most cases it is resolved. Repetitive dreams can indicate, especially if they've had the same basic theme, that the resolution is not yet at hand. If you dream of a horse which escapes from a stable, it tells you that the confinement is now over. The escape is a recognition that the containment is over and the release is complete. Look for this factor when interpreting your dreams. Sometimes, having the dream means that you are finished with that experience. Part of dream analysis deals with whether the dream is part of the solution or part of the problem. If it's repetitive, it's part of the problem; if it occurs only once, it's generally part of the solution.

Overall, it's very important to sift through the information after a night full of dreaming. Current research indicates that much of our dreaming time, whether it's when we sleep or when we daydream, has a lot to do with the creation of memory.

Imagine the brain as a computer that has to process the information that we acquire each and every day. It then evaluates the data in order to file it for future recall, discard it, or file it in another area of the brain, which we don't use on a daily basis. As the brain reviews all this information, we watch this process taking place in our dream state. We see these images being processed.

The images which stand out often have a lot to do with what is happening on the subconscious level. As you develop your psychic and intuitive abilities you will be able to discern between true subconscious feeling and the reviewing process that takes place to create memory. Once the desired images are distinguished from memory, you will have a door that opens straight into your inner self. Once in there, you can determine what fine-tuning is required to keep the lights burning bright.

CHAPTER FOUR

The DREAMER'S GUIDE

Chance encounters, unexpected coincidences
Premonitions, dreams and wishes
Flashes of unpredictable joy
Random events are
Weaving themselves in the web of time.

DEEPAK CHOPRA

O nce again I would like to emphasise that a dream dictionary cannot be formulated using the same principles one would use to create a language dictionary. Humans the world over have, in their own particular tongue, collectively created a word which conveys one, or in some cases, a number of meanings. In the English language, by agreement, the word 'school' means 'a place or sphere of activity that instructs'. However, if one dreamt of a school, it would be too simplistic to rush in and attach this definition within the context of the dream. Imagine the variety of meanings that can be attached; the person dreaming could be a school teacher or the dreamer could be a student still going to school. The interpretations of the dream would be at opposite ends of the spectrum. Compare the implications for a dreamer who has just left school with the dreamer who is a professional fisherman—his school might represent a school of fish.

In putting together the dreamer's guide listed in this chapter, I've been very careful not to influence your thinking too much. My desire is to merely show you the chords and allow you to write your own songs. To achieve this I have included the most common dream or daydream images and generalised how they might apply to you. I have also consulted other professionals and experts in their respective fields to ensure that the tools for self understanding are at your fingertips.

ANIMAL CRACKERS
IN MY SOUP

Most animal species have been on the planet a lot longer than humans. Therefore they must be given a certain amount of respect when they enter our dreams and daydreams. To understand what a particular animal in a dream indicates, look at what that animal represents to you. Is it a domestic pet? A predator? Is it impossible to control? Or does it just taste good? (Forgive me, if you are vegetarian.)

Let's take, for example, an owl. In Etruscan/Roman times the owl was the symbol of the healer and the builder, a wise person who commanded respect. The death of several Roman emperors was foretold by an owl alighting on the house, and hooting. In Greek mythology, the owl was sacred to the Earth

Goddess, Demeter. In native American traditions, the owl is recognised as a predator and a symbol of transformation, especially through the dark side or shadow of consciousness, as the owl is a nocturnal creature. It is sometimes called the night eagle and is a bird of sorcerers. In Asian traditions, the owl is thought by many to represent the possibility of a dangerous situation swooping into one's life. In China and Japan, in particular, many believe it signifies crime. In the Middle East the owl is seen as the embodiment of evil spirits and in Hebrew folklore it represents desolation, and is seen as unclean. In Celtic mythology the owl is a magical and sacred creature. In West African tribes the owl is seen as the messenger of wizards and its head is thought to be used for evil spells. Australian Aboriginals also believe the owl is the messenger of an evil deity. Yet the native Samoans believe that the owl, when seen in a dream, is a sacred symbol. In the West we know it as the symbol of wisdom.

Without a doubt it's very important to look at your cultural background and your experiences concerning the animal you have dreamt of, and then attach a personalised meaning to the symbol once you have taken into account the above considerations. You may, if you wish, expand on them. Don't let them limit you.

THE WALLS AROUND US

When I first thought about how to approach the subject of structures and buildings in dreams I scratched my head for a while and then it came to me (not in a dream, unfortunately). Why not go and speak to an architect? If anyone understands

Brett Ogle

I have a dream that has recurred on a few occasions. I'm lying on a grassy hill overlooking a lake, and the islands in the lake are the shapes of different countries. I know that I can get up and, by merely hopping, go to all the islands, but I don't get up because I'm glued to the grass.

buildings and structures within the imagination, surely it would be an architect.

Glynn Braddy is not only an architect, he is also a metaphysician. What follows is the essence of our discussion one sunny afternoon in the cool ocean breezes of Sydney's Manly beach.

In Western cultures there is almost a universal acceptance that your home, in a dream, is related to your body. Viewed esoterically, this means there is a close relationship between the building and human anatomy. The nature of the house is most often reviewed in the context of its different levels, for example, basement level, ground level, upper storey and attic space.

The basement generally refers to the subliminal aspects of the psyche. The lower zone can deal with one's innate sexuality, and the deeper sensual impulses of the unconscious of which the person is unaware, or prefers to remain unaware. It often deals with the base material, and the covert self where a person hides what they believe is 'wrong' with them. For women, it often deals with the feeling that they're not giving enough support, either to themselves, or to their family. In men, more often than not, the basement deals with their sexuality and their physical needs. For a female, the message is usually on an internal level, for a male, it is usually external. For females who dream of a basement flooding with water, it can mean an emotion is overtaking them. Yet males usually see it in darkness—the hidden creature of their darker impulses, at least in their minds.

The ground level deals more with what is occurring in one's current reality. It often deals with those things which are more pragmatic, more obvious, more accountable in a day. As most dreams deal with the ground level, they deal with what's happening at the conscious level, their nurturing, their sense of the world, and their day-to-day monetary self.

The upper level generally deals with intellect. A dream in which the house has a top floor usually deals with a person's identity in relation to their intellect and philosophy. Generally, people dream they're on an upper level from which they're looking at things from a higher perspective. They are trying to get to an altitude from where they can see an overall pattern. The further they go up, the more they begin to see that they're not living in an isolated field. There are many fields, and patterns of fields; they get to see the condition of the landscape generally. The philosophical self generally deals with achieving height and enlightenment from a higher perspective.

Above the top floor is the roof and attic space, which relate to a person expressing their spiritual aspirations, and are where the nature of a disciplined intellect gives access to the realm of transcendental perception.

Here is one of Glynn's upper level dreams to give you an example:

'I can recount, for instance, a dream I had once when I first became involved in meditation and biofeedback. I had a dream that I was climbing up a ladder in an attic and it seemed as if the attic went up, and somehow above there was a type of steeple, yet I could see stars through the top of it. As I was going up the ladder and I looked down and saw people standing around in the attic, I was saying 'C'mon, c'mon, there's no problem, it's safe.' But they were saying, 'No, I don't know, I don't think so.' I said, 'Look it's easy,' and I watched them actually going down the stairs and away. I realised I was going on to make a journey towards my highest aspirations, but I couldn't expect people to come with me. I couldn't expect them to think it was something they'd want to do. And I realised that somehow or other this would be a journey that I would make alone.'

PLACES OF WORSHIP

Fritz Perls' technique on how to interpret a dream by becoming the symbol is an excellent way to deal with places of worship. Simply become the place of worship you saw in your dream. Here are some examples which explains how it works.

1. I am Salisbury Cathedral and I have stood now for centuries. I am remarkable for my isolation, unlike a French cathedral or Italian cathedral where you are surrounded by a busy city. I am out in the field. I am dealing with separation and celibacy. The rain on me is wiping out the features of my wonderful sculpture. I have been allowed to fall into disrepair. But look! There are a lot of people working on my facade again. This would indicate that I am feeling a spiritual renewal and soon I will be appreciated for who I am.

2. I am Milan Cathedral in Italy. I see an Italian band with ostrich feathers and they are playing music at my gates, in front of the piazza. The locals are dressed vibrantly and dancing passionately. I am the centre of interaction between the people and the symbol of the divine. I am telling myself to loosen up—I can have fun and grow spiritually.

When interpreting dreams containing places of worship, it is often your feelings about the structure and how you perceive it in its surroundings rather than, 'Wow, I dreamt of a cathedral' that gives you the insight. Do you see it sparkling clean and new, or is it broken down and in need of repair? By addressing these questions you acknowledge that your subconscious is revealing to you your concern about your spine and your bones, and the ability to stand erect, your state of your spiritual foundations, or your personal life/relationships — what defines the interpretation is your intuition. For instance, if you see the cathedral in a state of disrepair yet packed to the rafters with individuals, the dream may indicate that you are a source of inspiration to many people without realising it. You may think that you are not together yet others think you are. Your subconscious is revealing what you may have perceived yet have not consciously acknowledged.

WORKPLACE

Generally speaking, if the structure is known to you — a workplace or an area where work is currently being conducted — it is more likely you are processing emotions and creating memory.

If it's an unfamiliar place of work, or a building or institution, then it could be telling you something different. The perception here could be around the desire to change, to achieve a situation more like the one in the dream. It may also indicate a lack of some of the ingredients of your current workplace.

For example, someone dreams they are working in a concrete office with bars on the windows and steel floors. They manage to cut a hole in the concrete and a ray of light seeps through. They put their eye to the hole and there's a forest with a beautiful waterfall. As this is not their office in reality, the meaning could be simple—they are looking for more environmentally friendly, healthy surroundings to express themselves. This is a simple example of one's relationship to the workplace and the need for a more abundant and creative experience.

THE TECHNICOLOUR DREAM

Individuals see colour differently. Each of us may have a different concept of what the three primary colours—red, yellow and blue—really look like. Science has shown that individuals may dream either in black and white or colour or both. Black and white dreams are usually connected with the emotions and events that you are dealing with on a day-to-day basis. Colour dreams usually come out of a deeper subconscious level. Although they may be more jumbled in content, they are certainly more vivid.

When interpreting the colours in your dream, put your own individual stamp on what the colour means to you. Colour choices—particularly your favourite colour—can be a guide to temperament, and the meaning of colour in a dream is very personalised. Traditionally, red means sexual drive and survival; orange means social interaction; yellow deals with intellect; green with compassion; turquoise with communication; blue with knowledge; violet with intuition; and magenta with the imagination or the spiritual. That's fine for traditional meanings, but what if you take a hypothetical situation where as a child red was linked to other meanings, such as, your red-headed babysitter dropped you on your head; a red-coated dog bit you on the way to preschool. If you drove through a red light and had an accident, red would mean danger to you rather than sexual drive, or survival. The point is, if a colour is vivid to you in a dream, discover what significance that colour has to you and perceive the associated vibration.

AROUND THE WORLD
IN 80 DREAMS

Dreaming that you're in a country other than the one you're living in, can afford some very interesting insights. It can indicate a craving on an unconscious level. I've said before that we are all psychic, and we all have unconscious intuition. This particular ability can be heightened when you do dream of foreign shores.

Firstly, examine the country that you have placed yourself in and write down what it represents to you, and the traditional way it is perceived now. Secondly, investigate the way it was perceived during its golden age and compare that to its present state.

For example, if you dream you're in Italy, how do you feel about Italy and Italians? What do you think of Rome during the height of the Roman Empire? What about during the Renaissance period and Italy's influence on the world today. Now, one at a time, see those emotions and perceptions as a backdrop to the rest of the elements of the dream.

Also explore the location you have landed in and the feelings that are associated with this experience. Following, are the sort of questions you can ask yourself to indicate your true feelings about changes — whether by travelling or other circumstances — that may be taking place in your life.

✠ How do I feel about the location — alienated or completely at home?

✠ Who was around me? Was I alone or did I travel with company? This can be particularly relevant if you normally travel alone and are accompanied by others in your dream and vice versa.

✠ The state of the location. Is it violent, peaceful, sunny, cold?

These questions can reveal to you the kind of change you either want to experience, or that you feel you may be being drawn into without any control. If you dream that you have arrived in a cold, bleak climate it may mean things are slowing down and that you are heading somewhere that is not going to give you comfort or abundance. Alternatively, you might want a more exciting, carefree existence and this could be indicated if you dream you are in a tropical island paradise. These two examples could also resemble your present spiritual state, it all comes down to individual intuition.

DREAMING OF THE PAST

The best thing about believing in past lives is—you can't lose. If there are past lives, you were right all the time and here we go again. If there is nothing after this lifetime, is doesn't matter, the lights go off and our mind shuts down. At least while the lights were on you lived with the comforting belief that there was something else. Either way let's go with the belief that there are past lives, and future lives as well. I am not going to talk about the piles of research and documentation that is available on past life recall during the dream state. If you care to look for the information you will find everything from the intriguing to the spine chilling. I believe it is more appropriate at this point to simply tell you what to look for if you feel you have had a past life experience contained in a dream.

If you wake up dressed up as a Roman centurion with a mouth full of grapes and a sign that says, 'I love Caesar', then you have just had a past life experience. But seriously, past life dreams do seem to be more real than the ones that are not. Reports show colours are brighter, they linger longer and are more likely to be three dimensional. Often, because there is so much to deal with, they reoccur. The best thing about past life dreams is the feeling you get, for it goes beyond the ego. When talking about past lives during the awakened state, people always say, 'I was this, I was that. I did this and I did that.' It's very egocentric. But when reporting a past life experience during a dream state, the 'I' is replaced by a feeling. More often people relate it in this manner: 'I felt Italian, I felt what it was like to be a female, I felt richer, poorer, limited . . .' The descriptive language is more about the feeling of the experience rather than the experience itself.

Finally, the best part about past life dreams is you're not usually Napoleon, Cleopatra or Alexander the Great. Once again you are simply Joe Citizen experiencing one of life's adventures, dealing with it and moving on.

DYING

Dying in a dream very rarely indicates that the dreamer or the person they're dreaming of is about to move on. What it usually indicates is transformation, change, or renewal, or perhaps a mental funeral for the problem they are currently wrestling with. Consider death in a dream as a purification process that must come before change can take place.

Stuart Wilde

I was on a train, dreaming in black and white. The train was moving up an incline. It seemed to struggle a bit but managed to make it to the top. The interesting thing about this dream was the train was empty when it started out on its journey, yet the further it moved up the hill, the more packed it became with people. By the time it got to the top it was full of people and the dream was in colour.

Another way to look at death in a dream is to look at the message behind the imagery. A good friend of mine Tom Mahas, world respected lecturer in the field of personal growth, once said to me, 'First you must choose how you want to die so that you know how you are going to live.' If someone dreams that they died at a ripe old age, healthy and content, surely it follows the message from the subconscious is, to achieve that end, let's get healthier, exercise more and be consciously optimistic.

FEELINGS

I believe that we only need to deal with four basic feelings in dreams: fear, frustration, joy and detachment.

Experiencing fear in dreams often comes about when someone feels they don't have the resources to deal with what's confronting them. Let's say you walk into a dark room and hear a hissing, growling sound in the opposite corner. You begin to experience fear of the unknown and fear that you may not have the resources to overcome the animal making the noises. You then switch on the light. If it's a six-month-old kitten your fear diminishes immediately because you feel you have the resources to overcome the kitten. If it's a Bengal tiger, fear continues and is magnified because you realise how limited your resources are. If you suddenly dream you have a 12-gauge shotgun in your hand and a key to open the door behind you, fear dissipates once again.

Frustration in dreams deals with a lack of fulfilment and satisfaction. It is the bed partner of fear. If you have enough frustration you can become afraid and if you have enough fear about something you'll feel frustrated. If you find yourself walking up the stairs but never reaching the top, frustration creeps in, then turns into fear if you feel you are going to run out of energy and fall all the way back down. What if a book suddenly appeared at your feet and you stopped climbing and started reading it? The frustration would disappear, and so would the fear.

Joy deals with levels of contentment and when this feeling is experienced in a dream, it has implications that happiness will follow. It could also indicate you are in very prosperous state but you may not be displaying this on a conscious level. Therefore your subconscious might be saying 'What's the struggle? What is there not to love? Count your blessings. You're doing okay.'

Detachment is experienced often during the dream state. This is a feeling of observation without any emotion attached to it. It's as if you are watching a movie about a subject that you have no attachment to. Whatever the outcome, it appears unimportant to you. When this state occurs in a dream, observe it knowing that it is as valid as the more obvious emotions like anger, fear, frustration and joy.

Detachment is a unique way of dealing with life situations occurring in both our sleeping and our waking state. Deepak Chopra, in his bestselling book *The Seven Spiritual Laws of Success*, describes the 'Law of Detachment' as being one of the most powerful keys to expanding your consciousness. He says that in order to acquire anything in the physical universe, you have to relinquish your attachment to it—not the actual intention or desire but the attachment to the result. He writes:

Relinquish your attachment to the known, step into the unknown, and you will step into the field of all possibilities. In your willingness to step into the unknown, you will have the wisdom of uncertainty factored in.

The search for security and certainty is actually an attachment to the known — our past. The known is nothing other than the prison of past conditioning. Uncertainty, on the other hand, is the fertile ground of pure creativity and freedom. This means that in every moment of your life, you will have excitement, adventure, mystery. When you are detached you are also less likely to force solutions on problems, which enables you to stay alert to opportunities. You can look at every problem you have in your life as an opportunity for some greater benefit. Anything you want can be acquired through detachment, because detachment is based on the unquestioning belief in the power of your true Self.

The Law of Detachment can easily be applied to dream interpretation and the way dreams are viewed as a whole. By observing from the grandstand, rather than playing the game, one experiences the comfort required in order to stay in the dream state and remain in control. Therefore, because of the radical nature of our dream adventures, we can enjoy the security of exploring unbounded territory, view its liberating qualities and apply these to our conscious life in order to experience the unlimited field of possibilities.

TASTY DREAMS

Food is a substance that can be taken into a living organism and converted to energy and body tissue. If something is that important in our waking life, then we should consider giving it similar respect during a dream state. I ask myself the following questions: Am I getting enough? Am I satisfied with the amount placed before me? Am I feeding someone or am I being fed? What does it taste like?

Here is an example, let's say you dreamt that your mother came to your workplace, took a large meal from your employer's desk, put it in front of you and then you began to eat it. Applying the above questions, it would be pretty safe to assume that there is a message from your subconscious telling you that deep down you feel that, in the job in which you are currently employed, the environment or the people do not supply you with a creative sense of fulfilment. It also tells you that someone who has nurtured you in the past supports this theory and it could be time to move on or reassess your direction. I maintain that the symbolic presence of food in dreams is an integral part of the total interpretation.

C.O.D.
(CASH ON DREAMING)

I believe that money is the root of all pleasure. Perceptions like 'Money is the root of all evil' and someone being 'filthy rich' are negative. If you remove all guilt around abundance you can move a long way towards understanding the true nature of this particular energy.

The one thing that gives us dignity is choice. The more choices, the more dignity, and the more abundance, the more choices. What I'm saying is, it's okay to feel good about money or abundance in a dream.

If you dream you earn money, lose money, receive it or give it away, look at the money in the dream as a form of energy which individuals around the world have agreed is valuable. When you think about it, it's really a fancy piece of printing or a piece of plastic that we are exchanging between ourselves. The value, or the energy, can be translated into choices.

I want you to expect that things are going to sustain you. Why shouldn't they? Life sustains itself. Get used to beginning to work on your feelings so that you come out of a powerful energy, a feeling of abundance. That feeling of abundance has nothing to do with how much money you've got. Abundance is saying: 'I feel rich in my feelings, I feel rich in the friendships I have, in the love I have, in my intellect; I feel abundant in nature, in the naturalness of all things; I feel strong, and the fact that I may not have a pot to piss in is a mere aberration.' Once you feel abundant you are bound to become it, and that's the secret.

Stuart Wilde

DREAM TUNES

If you dream of music and song, consider the tune and the person playing the musical instrument more than the meaning of the instrument itself. However, if you are a musician, then the considerations are more in keeping with what abundance and profile the instrument is providing for you.

If you do not play a musical instrument, consider that there could be a relationship between seeing the musical instrument and a hidden desire to develop a creativity that will make you more visible. If someone else is playing the musical instrument, consider that they may be looking for attention. Perhaps they are waiting for you to make the first move, or perhaps they require a reaction from you.

MOTHER NATURE
AND THE SEASONS

When attempting to interpret dreams, if you are fortunate enough to remember the season during which the dream took place, you are blessed with an extra level of understanding. Regard the meaning of the season and that should afford you a greater insight into the dream.

Spring: A time for new ideas, a blossoming, nurturing, the start of new things, the early manifestation, perhaps an awakening.

Summer: A time of the harvest, collective effort, the orchestration of human endeavours, more light, heat, holidays, a vast supply of the fruits of nature.

Autumn: A time for things to fall away but preceded by an expression in the most brilliant way in the physical, a time of a final display of life before moving on, the last moments, a sense of things coming to an end.

Winter: A time of hibernation, darkness, imagining, internalising, solitude. A season where you can't expect to see things grow or blossom, a time for an inner, unseen development, a time of potential energy.

Add to these concepts the way you feel about the season. Do you always look forward to summer because it means you take your annual holidays or do you dread summer because it also means school holidays and more responsibilities? Does spring mean a never-ending number of sneezes or, if you're a gardener, a time when finally all your hard work begins to blossom? Examine the seasons closely and their personal meaning for you.

Denise Robert, star of the ABC-TV hit series, G.P. had a macabre dream which turned out to be prophetic:

While I was running a disco in Papua New Guinea, I would wake in a cold sweat from a frequent dream in which I saw myself lying dead in a coffin.

Add these ideas as you would to any puzzle that you are trying to piece together. Seeing the links can help you understand the big picture.

Nature scenes contained in dreams often speak for themselves. They represent quiet solitude and a space that is safe and rejuvenating. If this is the case with your inner feelings, then it's simple enough to comprehend why you've placed yourself within a nature atmosphere. However, if you're totally bored with this type of scene, and you want to chop it down or want to be removed from it, consider why something in its natural state offends you. Investigate why dramatic change is so important to you and the concept of natural evolution may cause some irritation.

In closing, may I say that when nature calls, go.

ARE YOUR NUMBERS UP?

Numbers in a dream have a lot to do with the personal association they may have in your life. For instance, the number of your house, your lucky number or even that magical number your favourite sporting hero wears. Numbers are as specific and personal to the dreamer as any other symbol.

It has been my experience that there are often three people in a dream or three of something. The three symbols tend to represent three different aspects of the dreamer—the spiritual side, the physical and the psychological. The insight here is to understand how they point to a different areas of oneself and what the message is for that particular element. Intuitively select the symbol that represents the mind, then the body and the spirit. If the one you've chosen to represent the mind is slow, lethargic and bogged down, then there's an obvious message there. If the one that represents the spirit is in prison or subdued, the conclusion again is obvious. If growth and vitality are displayed in the symbol for the body it can represent a positive affirmation that you believe you are on the right track in this area.

Paying attention to numbers can be very significant. If it's your desire to understand in more detail to what extent numbers can influence life, I recommend both David A. Phillips' and Robin Stein's work, details of which are in the Further Reading section at the end of this book.

FROM ANKLES TO ARMPITS

We often use parts of the body to metaphorically communicate our feelings, for example, 'They are a pain in the neck', 'I'll give you a helping hand', 'That sticks in my throat', 'It touches my heart', 'I'd like to get this off my chest', 'Seeing eye to eye'. If you dream of a particular part of the body, either your own or someone else's, there is usually an underlying meaning to the image.

I work with these images in the following way. Firstly, I look at whether it's my body, someone else's body, or if it's part of an animal. Secondly, I reflect upon how I am affected by that part of the body, or how I (or the other person or animal) is affected by that body. Thirdly, I examine how the demobilisation or enhancement affects them or myself. Finally, I look for a meaning attached to my conclusions.

Here is an example: You dream of a horse in a bare field. The horse looks like it is injured and is hobbling. You approach the horse and turn its hoof over to see a stone is lodged there causing the pain and impediment. You don't know how to remove it but a local farmer with a kind face appears and removes the stone. The horse then runs off into a distant, lush meadow to eat the grass. This is a simple analogy that could mean a small yet noticeable object is holding you back from progress and full potential in your work. You are unable to remove the obstruction yourself but someone kind who understands the limitation gives you the assistance you need to move on into greener pastures. Being able to accept help from others may also be part of this process.

BEANS,
HUMAN BEANS THAT IS

How do you feel about the people in your dreams? Look at what they represent to you, their occupation, their age and their general state of wellbeing. Are they related to you? Are they associated with you in business? Do you admire them? And so on. Pay particular attention to the way they appear in the dream. Were they taller or shorter than they are in real life? Fatter or thinner? If their occupation was different in the dream to their actual real-life occupation, make a note of that. Try to remember the way they were dressed.

When gauging how you feel about them within the dream, compare that feeling to how you feel about them in everyday life. Did you trust them in the dream, did they make you feel good? Why did you bring them up at this very intimate moment in your life? What about strangers? You've never seen these people and in this instance you must rely on the emotions you felt when you saw them. Were they enticing or hostile? Did they attract you or repulse you? Then, once you've established that emotion, determine what part is attracting you, is repulsing you, is hostile to you or is enticing you. If they're famous people like movie stars, politicians or people who are in the media, besides considering how you feel towards them, look at their profession and what that represents to you. If they are movie stars, recall the last movie in which you saw them. Take all these factors into consideration.

For example, if you dreamt you went to dinner with Tom Cruise your interpretation would differ depending on whether the last movie you had seen was *Far and Away* or *A Few Good Men*. If you dreamt about someone in the music industry, also take into account any song which that individual performed which has had an impact on you in some way.

Finally, if you dream about anyone, you may choose to simply find one word to describe that person. Then apply that one word as an element of yourself in the context of the dream you are interpreting. For instance, the person may be exemplifying generosity. If you recognise that trait it could mirror your own generous character.

MOBILE DREAMS

Modern technology has given humans the ability to travel to any place on the planet. Although we can't physically fly higher than an eagle or run faster than a cheetah, with the aid of mechanical devices we can do a lot better.

When travelling or moving in a dream, it is important to see the result of the journey as much as the implements or technology used to make it. Flying in an aeroplane, sitting in a car or riding a bicycle, have their traditional meanings. However, what I like to review are the following: Why I got on the plane, in the car or on the bike; how secure I felt with these devices; did they get me there quicker, slower, more comfortably, or safely; and how did I feel when I got there?

For example, if you dreamt that you got on your brother's bike to get to the beach, putting aside how you feel about your brother or not having your own bike, just look at the fact that you needed to pedal your way quickly to the ocean to perhaps cool down. Consider aspects such as you need to get to a place where you can relax and cool off quickly, not so much 'What does bike mean to me?'

Allow some variation if you are a technician or tradesperson who works with aeroplanes, cars, bikes and so on, or if you have a person close to you who works with these means of transport. In this instance the symbols can imply more about your feelings related to the work completed, or the time it takes to complete the maintenance of the transportation system, rather than the actual transportation system.

In Western culture, the motor vehicle has become so important to our very existence. It represents mobility, convenience, reliability or unreliability, but most of all, it is used every day. You could take the motor car if it's your own vehicle as a representation of self. Traditionally, your home can be a representation of yourself, however, in this day and age your motor vehicle is a similar representation.

DAYTIME FRIENDS
AND NIGHT TIME LOVERS

The good news is that your dream lovers are really aspects of yourself that you want to accentuate. If you dreamt you were making love to Jerry Seinfield, it's the humorous, irreverent and the subtly sarcastic side of yourself that you want to bring out and connect with. If it's Sylvester Stallone, it's the physical and adventurous part of yourself that you are making love to. If it's Marilyn Monroe, then it could be that you feel it's time to be more sensual and desirable. Whomever or whatever your dream lover, it is what that person symbolises to you that you wish to embrace, and in the embrace there is the possibility of becoming more like the qualities of your dream lover. There should never be any guilt attached to having regular dream lovers, or many and varied dream lovers. There is no point in feeling unfaithful or weird. It is as simple as this: dream lovers are you in another form, playing a role you wish to become more like. Have fun with them, enjoy them and look at them for what they are; an aspect of yourself that you wish to awaken.

UNIVERSAL SYMBOLS

As I discussed in Chapter Two, no-one can truly interpret the meaning of a dream by using a dream dictionary. It is just too simple to say an apple always means health, bread means success, and flying means movement. At the risk of being tedious, let me illustrate one more time using the dream subject of water. It's generally accepted that water means emotions and spirituality. But what if you were a sailor in the merchant navy. It's going to mean work and separation. If you were a sailor in the Royal Navy it could mean adventure or even danger. If you are a fisherman it is more likely to signify tranquillity and peace. I am sure you see my point, dream interpretation is a very personal exploration.

But even though the thought of a dream dictionary makes me cringe, I am reluctantly forced to admit that there is a place for universally accepted symbol meanings. No matter where you travel in the world, everyone will agree that two golden arches means food and five coloured rings represents the Olympics. We have mutually agreed to communicate by way of symbols, gestures and sounds that are universally understood.

Symbols are the language of dreams. The subconscious mind speaks in symbols, forming imagery and scenarios that you can work with and understand.

Let's divide symbols into three basic types—the personal, conventional, and archetypal. The personal interpretation of dreams and their importance is what this book is all about. The conventional and the archetypal I have placed less importance on, but it would be remiss of me to exclude them altogether.

The conventional group are images and symbols so specific that they mean the same thing to everyone. For example, the printed face of George Washington on a green piece of paper means a dollar to everyone. So too, there are instances where the most obvious perception of the symbol is the meaning behind the dream.

Archetypal symbols and images are universal on a subconscious level. They are what Carl Jung refers to as part of the 'collective unconscious'. They are the energy behind all other images and symbols. To put it simply, Jung believed that people

Kerri-Anne Kennerley

I had the strangest dream once. I was inside an oyster shell and from inside this shell I could hear all the other oysters around me being opened up. Finally, someone picked me up. They opened the shell but instead of finding me in there, they found a pearl.

throughout the world have a shared understanding of archetypes. These are the embodiment of the world's collective history passed on subconsciously through the generations. Some examples of archetypal symbols and their meanings include priestesses and healing, knights and chivalry, wizards and magic, kings and leadership. Even though I've often said, 'How can apples mean the same to all of us?' the fact remains that the majority of humankind would come with the same response, 'Apples have something to do with health and wellbeing.'

So without any further ado, and at the insistence of my publisher, editor and proofreaders, here is the mandatory dreamer's guide section that makes all dream books complete. I have selected what I believe are the most common symbols along with a couple of general suggestions and pointers to spark your imagination. Place your own suggestions in the dreamer's guide, too.

DREAMER'S GUIDE

Aeroplane: Take off; lofty thoughts; detachment; change.

Aliens: Aloneness; bureaucratic cover-up; superior intelligence.

Alligator: Able to live in two worlds at once; amphibious.

Amputation: Less mobility; letting go.

Angel: Guides; protection; support; messengers.

Antiques: The past; valuable; ancestors; security.

Applause: Acknowledgement; completion; joy; relief.

Apple: Forbidden fruit; health; acknowledgement.

Appointment: Commitment; decisions; structure.

Army: Power; comradeship; service; protection.

Arrow: Freedom; on target; penetrating; direct; confrontation.

Baby: New consciousness; commitment.

Baggage: Control; encasement; burdens; transformation.

Balcony: Clear vision; romance; release; unconfined.

Ball: Movement; indecision; desire; focus.

Banquet: Abundance; over-indulgence; celebration; acknowledgement.

Barefoot: Connection; non-conforming; danger; unrestricted.

Beach: Meeting point; recreation; rejuvenation.

Bees: Sweetness; work; prosperity; hidden pain.

Birds: Higher consciousness; liberty; mobility. (It is important to note type of bird.)

Birth: Beginning; creation; change.

Blindness: Closed-mindedness; greater care.

Blood: Power; life; fear; dedication.

Book: Knowledge; wisdom; learning.

Bread: Nourishment; abundance; fulfilment.

Bridges: Connection; transcendence; support.

Butterfly: Transformation; completion; fulfilment.

Candle: Illumination; peace; celebration; overworked.

Cat: Independence; long life; suspicion; two-faced.

Cave: Withdrawal; hibernation; mystery; safety.

Chains: Control; restraint; linking.

Chocolates: Love; passion; temptation.

Climbing: Ascending; achievement.

Clocks: Realisation; remembering the moment; moving on.

Clouds: Ungrounded; undefined; hidden softness; distance.

Computer: Power; control; work; image of one's own mind.

Cook: Provider; benefactor; manifestator; transformer.

Crowds: Agreement; alignment; social.

Crown: Power; authority; wealth.

Crystal: Unseen energy; beauty; precious; special power.

Cup: Reservoir; containment; practical; nourishment.

Dance: In step; confirming; creativity; relief; expression.

Desert: Shifting; resourceful; barren; travel.

Dog: Loyalty; faithfulness; protection.

Doors: New possibilities; new openings; change.

Eggs: Soul; new life; nurturance. (Note what form they take: sunny-side up, in a nest, scrambled.)

Falling: Unsupported; ungrounded; lack of focus.

Fantasy: A mirror of self; release of passion.

Fire: Purification; heat; passion.

Flag: Belonging; unifying; reverence.

Flower: Growth; connection with nature; spring.

Foreign Country: Movement; past life; new experiences ahead.

Garden: Sanctuary; peace; cultivation.

Gold: Abundance; power; precious.

Grapes: Intoxication; indulgence; abundance; versatility.

Heaven: Peace; rest; judgement.

Hell: Punishment; undesirable results.

Hospital: Healing; danger; antiseptic.

Invitation: Commitment; opportunity; respect; networking.

Island: Solitude; haven; detachment; single-mindedness.

Jewels: Possession; loyalty; hidden treasure; desire.

Jungle: Undisciplined; adventure; unknown; survival.

Kitchen: Satisfaction; transformation; family connection; hospitality.

Kiss: Affection; farewell; success; loud rock band.

Ladder: Achievement; power; ascendancy. (It's important to note what direction you are heading.)

Lake: Surrounded; rejuvenation; hidden emotions.

Marriage: Union; bonding; commitment; loss of identity.

Mermaid: Temptation; sensuality; adaptability.

Mirrors: Reflecting; confronting; empathy.

Moon: Femininity; spirituality; cycles; tides; mother.

Mountains: Challenges; lofty ideals; goals.

Naked: Freedom; exposure; sensuality.

Navel: Birth; connection with nature; life-line.

Oyster: Hidden wealth; antagonism; lack of mobility; indulgence.

Pen: Communication; authority; messages; expression.

Perfume: Enticement; camouflage; warning; hiding.

Poison: Change; trickery; indigestible.

Pregnant: New life; manifestation of project; co-dependency.

Rainbow: Celebration; change; optimism.

Ring: Union; fidelity; eternity.

River: Life; movement; flowing.

Roads: Possibilities; adventure; departures.

Rock: Strength; stability; solid.

Running: Escape; movement; exercise.

Sacrifice: Guilt; martyrdom; ritual.

Sailing: Controlling; travel; resolution.

School: Learning; discipline; youth.

Sex: Making love to an aspect of self.

Shoes: Privilege; mobility; prosperity.

Sneezing: Release; agitation; danger.

Soil: Power; grounding; solid; reliable.

Spiders: Intrigue; entangled; trapped.

Stairs: Possibilities; success; achievement.

Star: Faraway places; guidance; light; perception.

Storms: Turbulence; anger; release.

Sun: Power; warmth; father; masculine.

Teeth: Youth; health; functional; power.

Trees: Growth; connection; life; ancestry.

Tunnel: Narrow-mindedness; passageways.

Watch: Control; order; discipline; knowledge.

Water: Spirituality; emotions; replenishment; vital.

Windows: New horizons; looking outwardly; openness.

In closing, I would just like to remind you that these symbol definitions are simply a guide; a stepping stone to the lofty heights of understanding the meanings behind your dreams. They will simply help you to wake up to yourself.

Oscar-winning Australian cinematographer,
Dean Semler, whose films include DANCES
WITH WOLVES, YOUNG GUNS and THE MAN
FROM SNOWY RIVER was puzzled by a
recurring dream:

*I saw myself falling continually and I tried to
save myself by grabbing at a scaffold which my
camera was mounted on. My film crew were
dangling like monkeys from the scaffold,
reaching out to me with their free hands, but I
could not reach them.*

SUMMARY

We all have intuition. Through this intuition we have the ability to understand the images we see when the unconscious mind passes messages to the conscious mind. If we don't understand them immediately, that's fine, because an individual may be at an evolutionary point of life when it doesn't serve them to know. When the time is right, the required inspiration will be forthcoming and the interpretation will have clarity.

In the meantime, continually work on the meaning of symbols and relate them to the way you feel today. Update your personal dream dictionary as often as possible. If, for example, you wrote a notation under 'kitchen' a year ago when it was old and dilapidated, notice how the meaning of the symbol changes once the kitchen is refurbished and you don't need to deal with tradespeople and disruptions. Finally, months later when you've had a successful dinner party, the meaning of 'kitchen' changes again because all the drama is forgotten and you associate 'kitchen' with successful entertaining.

I can't emphasise enough how important it is to change the -meanings you attach to symbols in a dream as often as you can. I would like to emphasise four points which are the foundations of individual dream interpretation.

1. Dreams are a very private and individual experience, most of which should never be verbalised or shared with another individual. If you do make the decision to discuss a dream with someone, it should be on the condition that it is kept as confidential as possible.

2. The only dream dictionary to refer to is the one that you've written yourself. Update it regularly and don't let anyone else borrow it or use it.

3. Don't worry if you can't remember your dreams. Work on it, develop your ability slowly, and it will come to you in time as you put a greater value on remembering your dreams.

4. When reviewing a dream, go over it in the present tense, for example, 'I am running down the hill, I am now turning the corner and drinking the water,' and so on. Use as much colourful, expressive and creative language as possible.

CHAPTER FIVE

DREAM AEROBICS

You now come to this playhouse of infinite forms.

DEEPAK CHOPRA

O ne day while working out at the gym, I had a thought. If by continual exercise I am able to build up my muscles, and become fitter, what if the same applied to my ability to interpret dreams? If I continually develop my interpretative skills and my psychic abilities, with the same dedication that I put into maintaining my physical fitness, then surely I will see measurable results. With this premise in mind, I have put together five dreams which are not typical dreams. There's no special significance to any of them; they're just exercises for the mind the same as weightlifting is exercise for the muscles. They are designed to develop your intuition in your own dream interpretation and to practise with until you have your own dream on which you want to work. Also, in between your dreams, you might try these exercises, just to keep your imagination at its sharpest.

Complete these exercises, then finish reading this book. Allow at least six months to pass, then open this chapter again and revise the exercises. I believe you will be surprised how different your perceptions and interpretations around the symbols will be.

There are no right or wrong answers. I know you'll enjoy the process of coming to your own conclusion. Make the experience of understanding the messages contained in the dreams simple and effortless. If you require more exercises, look at books that recount dreams, but don't look at the analysis until you have had time to come to conclusions of your own. Better still, wait until your next dream and have fun with that.

EXERCISE ONE

You dream that you are speeding down a highway in your car. Two police officers speed past you and pull you over to the side of the road. You have stopped in front of a beautiful beach that has huge waves pounding on the shore. One of the police officers leans in the window and hands you a glass of water that you spill all over your red T-shirt. Write down your interpretations for the following symbols:

Driving:

Highway:

Your car:

The number two:

Police officer:

Oceans:

Glass of water:

Red T-shirt:

I think dreams are a gift from God to show us what is possible for us in all levels of consciousness. For one-third of our lives we are able to go into a pure, dimensionless state, to leave this body and enter a dreaming body where there is no doubt, to teach us that it's possible to live without doubt. Dreams teach us that the waking state is our illusion.

Dr Wayne Dyer

EXERCISE TWO

You are crawling around the foundations under your home, looking for a light switch. Instead you find a ladder which takes you from the foundations to the roof where you see a candle and light it, causing nine bats to fly out towards the moon. Write down your interpretations of the following symbols:

Basement:

Light switch:

Crawling:

Ladder:

Roof:

Candle:

Light:

Nine bats:

Moon:

Flying:

A dream is a state of consciousness, just like deep sleep. Dreams can give you hindsight into experiences occuring for you in space/time reality. Dream experiences can be valid and interesting if we can use them within our other states of consciousness, such as the waking state.

Dr Deepak Chopra

EXERCISE THREE

You arrive home after a party. Some people, whom you met at the party but didn't know previously, want to keep dancing in your loungeroom. They turn on your sound equipment, begin to eat all your food, take all your clothes off, then make you leave because you're not laughing enough. Your dog comes in, sniffs in each corner of the room and then they disappear. Write down your interpretations of the following symbols:

Home:

Party:

Loungeroom:

Dancing:

Sound equipment:

Food:

Nakedness:

Laughter:

Dog:

Sniffing:

Disappearance:

Dreams are the subconscious speaking to us, and it tells us how much we can take and how much we can change.

Shirley Maclaine

EXERCISE FOUR

You are down at the beach lying in the sun, when five individuals invite you to take your costume off, as they have done, and dive into the surf. As you frolic in the water, one of these individuals begins to make love to you. You are unable to relax and enjoy it because you are conscious of the other four looking at you. You ask them would they like to take your place. Write down your interpretations of the following symbols:

Beach:

Lying:

Sun:

Five people:

Nakedness:

Making love:

Offering:

Focus of attention:

Emotion:

A person gets an impression from a dream and the impression is lasting even though sometimes the details are not. Use your intuitive ability, hang on to the impression and don't just take one detail as gospel.

Robin Stein

EXERCISE FIVE

Your parents walk you to school, but instead of the school there is a familiar place of worship. You refuse to go in, run away and hide behind a waterfall on the other side of a cemetery. Inside a cave, there is an old man wearing an orange sari and playing a flute. He doesn't say anything. He just smiles and continues with his music. Write down your interpretations of the following symbols:

Mother/father:

School:

Place of worship:

Running:

Cemetery:

Waterfall:

Old man:

Orange:

Flute:

Everything we do has a purpose and a lesson for us through which to grow and evolve. We have a choice to grow a little each lifetime or stay here and get it all done, making the very best of what we have.

David A. Phillips

Steve (Blocker) Roach

My most memorable dreams are ones where I am surrounded by my family and friends while picnicking or relaxing in a garden. I wake up feeling warm and content because I'm surrounded by lots of children.

 CHAPTER SIX

The DREAM SHUFFLE and the TAROT DECK

Through Myriad eyes
You see yourself.

DEEPAK CHOPRA

O pinion is divided as to when exactly tarot cards first appeared in the West. One popular theory is that they are the essence of esoteric wisdoms of the ancient Egyptians, other researchers claim they were brought to the West by gypsies. It is well-documented that Jung, after his life-long dedication to dream research, came to the conclusion that the core of our dream imagery was the source of the symbols recorded in the tarot.

Throughout time, the tarot has been closely related to the dream state and it thus offers a tool for self development. The cards in themselves do not have any intrinsic power. The power comes from the individual's ability to comprehend a relevant message. Once your psychic skills have been developed, the cards can act as a window into your mind, providing clearer images of your inner nature and the choices that are available to you.

The following technique, which I call the Dream Shuffle, may be useful as part of your repertoire when interpreting your dreams. Select any tarot deck that you are drawn to. There are many decks available on the market, so choose one that you feel a connection with.

The process in itself is quite simple. Create a quiet space for yourself free from any interruptions. You may wish to burn essential oils that promote intuitive qualities in a vaporiser, light a candle and play some empowering music in the background. In this intuitive state you have created for yourself, refer to the following pages which list the meaning of the 21 major tarot cards. For example, read the meaning of the tenth card, the Wheel of Fortune, and start to feel the energy of what this card is signifying.

THE DREAMER'S SHUFFLE

Using the major cards as a dream symbol can be very significiant. Separating them from the rest of the pack, you can either use the cards to interpret and understand a dream, or pick a card to visualise on in order to begin a dream. Through practice you will be able to do both with skill and expertise, your doorway between worlds will open up and you will be able to see past, present and future simultaneously.

Shuffle the major card deck and think of the dream, reviewing it in the present tense. When the reviewing process is complete, cut the deck into three piles forming a triangle. Turn over the pile at the apex of the triangle to reveal the bottom card. Begin to write about the images you see on the card, looking for all the details and describing the imagery. The guide below will help with the interpretation. Use the feeling and emotions you are transcribing as a catalyst to unlock the hidden meaning you are searching. If you require verification or more detail, you can turn either of the two remaining piles of the triangle. I suggest, wherever possible, to work on the first card only—first impressions are usually the most accurate.

While this system has absolutely no scientific basis, if you are willing to believe that every one of us has intuitive powers, then the Dream Shuffle can be developed into a useful tool for inspirational answers. If you wish to further explore the tarot or other intuitive sciences there are many wonderful books on the subject and I also humbly recommend *Cards, Stars & Dreams* which provides a comprehensive guide to the tarot including the major and minor cards. (Descriptions following correspond to the Rider Waite Tarot deck.)

The Fool

This is a great card. It's telling you to loosen up and not take life so seriously. Life's too short to be so serious. Look at the wisdom contained in comic relief and in sarcasm. Get out of situations with humour rather than sheer brute force.

Jesters of the courts would relieve tension and pressure by making fun of a situation and bringing it out in the open, and everyone, from the king down, would have a good laugh. Lighten up, loosen up and also pay homage to those individuals who are able to make you laugh. Have a shot at laughing at everything you believe.

The Fool is also symbolic of children and babies, innocence and simplicity. Children are so honest and straight to the point, there's none of the clutter. Over-analysis of your dream is not necessary, just see it simply as it is.

The Fool indicates that it is a time to trust, express naturalness, happiness and laughter, and enjoy new beginnings and choices. It can mean the birth of a baby. Approach your dream with a new freshness, and trust that all will work out fine.

The Magician

This is a reminder of your unique magic. Everyone is magical, full of resources and has the ability to create whatever they want in their lives. Don't forget that you are a powerful individual, you are infinite, you are immortal, you are universal. If you forget that, you feel your choices are limited, but it's not true. You have many different options, it doesn't matter what problem you have or what you are doing with it at the moment, there are always a number of choices if you want to sit down and think about it. There's simply one road to journey down, and the 'magician' in you can conjure up the path for you. You may not be able to wave the magic wand, changing things instantly, but you can certainly walk towards a solution. Always remember the three things that go hand in hand. Firstly, there is the thought, then there's the word and then there's action. You can think it, you can verbalise it and then you can do something about it.

You can talk about things, but without action what's the point? You can tell people they have the power and resources within them to do whatever they want, but many people do not know how to access this power. It's truly great to know that you are powerful, but now what? It's important to bring an idea into the physical and motivate it into action.

The Magician indicates a time to make decisions. Mastering your mind and controlling your life are the issues at hand. What tools do you need to create your life? If you are a man, this card can represent youth; if a woman, desire. Use the cards of the tarot to enrich and add meaning to your dream.

The High Priestess

There's a need to feel more gentleness and spirituality in your life. Bring more love into your life. Touch on the feminine side of yourself and hang out with the matriarchs in your life—sit down and listen to what they have to say and how they feel, and see how it affects your life. (This applies to both sexes.) It's time to get in touch with the feminine and femininity.

It may be the moment to connect to all that is feminine, mysterious and deep. Psychic development is taking place. If you are a woman, this card can represent youth; if a man, desire. Intuition is the key to unlocking your dream.

The Empress

The Empress indicates the power behind mother nature, the power behind all things. There is an Emperor sitting there running the empire, but behind the Emperor is the Empress with the big stick.

Perceive things behind the obvious. Just because someone is screaming at you for not doing your job right, it doesn't mean they're angry with you. What they could be trying to convey is a commitment from you to do a better job. They want you to succeed and if you're able to look beyond the anger, then you can perfect your skills. Always think of the motives behind, or the intentions behind, a situation. The real strength may be with the Emperor, but it's the Empress who is holding it all together.

Realise you are in a very fertile stage in your life, sexually or mentally, and you could be feeling inspired and full of ideas. Don't simply look at fertility in the physical sense, look at it in the creative sense as well, and if you are thinking of new projects and new inventions, bring it into form right now. It's a time to nurture your ideas into being.

The Empress represents motherhood, getting in touch with your femininity, balancing that with your masculinity (the Emperor), and expressing that with a partner.

You may feel the need for mothering or to be mothered. It is a time to connect to your own creativity or to an expression that comes from deep within. Can indicate a birth, pregnancy or your mother.

The Emperor

I would seek the counsel of someone who is wise about either your dream or the situation you were working with in the dream. The Emperor holds a position of power not solely because of heredity. They are also usually well-educated and capable of seeing the big picture, just as someone in your family or someone you know may.

Sam Neill

I have a recurring dream that really intrigues me. It's in black and white, and I'm in my classroom at school surrounded by individuals from my past, all of whom I have no contact with today.

The Emperor portrays authority and is the take charge card. It shows someone offering insights into dream aspects. In regard to your dream, the Emperor is about taking charge of where you are going, and can represent the need to become more powerful. May mean a positive change in the direction of your life. Can represent your father.

The Hierophant

If you are looking for spiritual confirmation, acknowledgement or permission for what you are doing and you pulled this card up, it means you don't need it. You are the Pope of your own church, you are the High Priestess, you are the Priest and you are the congregation. All your spiritual needs and decisions come from within.

We're referring to spiritual needs here, and while people can join an organised religion to satisfy a certain need, to satisfy a spiritual need, one needs to go within. It's time you stopped searching for outside approval. The one person who knows you better than anyone else is yourself.

The Hierophant shows a need to contact inner wisdom and not external advice on dream symbolism, but it can also mean a need to structure what's already been going on. I would say it's time to choose a new path, a new way of doing something. It's time to restructure. The Hierophant represents the time to search for true spiritual meaning in tradition and traditional values. A therapist and/or teacher may enter your life to show you your path. It is a time to study something new.

The Lovers

There is a volcano inside you that is waiting to erupt, a passion inside you that wants to be loved, wants to love, wants to give and wants to receive. There's the symbolism of forbidden fruit in this card. Adam would do anything for Eve's love, to the point of eating the forbidden fruit. I'm not judging Adam, I'm simply mentioning it as an observation. Do not give up everything you've got so you can hold on to a partner. Your partner should love you, warts and all, and you shouldn't have to give up everything.

The Lovers card is very much a representation of Adam and Eve and the garden of Eden. Snake is sexual passion and the fire represents sexual tension. You must let the whims of individuality dance between you, and not embrace to the point where you are not being yourself.

Can represent a time to generate self love. (Dispense with trying to change someone after you've fallen in love with them.) It's very symbolic that the woman in the card is looking at the angel which allows divinity and spirituality, and the man is looking at the woman. It represents biological urges and spirituality. The spirituality of love is something that you can generate; it's a feeling and a need.

The Lovers can indicate a connection to your dream lover. Also, being open to warm and loving relationships. Be aware of communication difficulties with those close to you. You may hear of a marriage.

The Chariot

The Chariot speaks of the conflict within, the male and female, the yin and yang. There are two opposing views within you. Will I, won't I? Should I, shouldn't I? Am I, am I not? Unless you can balance these you'll topple over. You have to manage the two opposing views so they pull with equal force and strength in order for you to move along. Harness both sides with equal power and stop procrastinating. Once you've done this, you can get the result you desire. Make a decision and go for it without necessarily disenfranchising one or the other. Move on with speed by giving encouragement to both views. Remember, if you're not sure where you are going, every single road will take you there.

A dream is pulling you in two different directions. The whole card implies control and making decisions, and not making a decision is still a decision. The Chariot represents a need for direction. At the moment you are holding the whole situation together with will power.

This card can symbolise your inner drives and ambitions, and the need for goals that are achievable. It may represent being torn in two different directions. This will need to be resolved before you can move ahead.

Strength

Strength doesn't necessarily mean brute force. There's strength in humility, there's strength in patience, there's strength in subtlety, strength in love and hope. Don't be fooled by the obvious display of strength, the obvious display of power. You can be strong when you are silent, you can be strong by walking away, you can be strong by nurturing, by seeing the other side of the equation. Strength is eternal — the infinity symbol — there's strength in living to fight another day.

Strength comes not so much from a show of power; the key word to strength is endurance. How many people do you know who are in situations they don't like but are in anyway because of some type of discipline or honour?

In a passive sense, this card could also mean you may have 'tamed the lion'; that is, tamed your inner desires. It represents the need for self discovery and a time to get in touch with how you really feel. Trust your inner intuitive nature.

The Hermit

This is an indication that you need time out and solitude. Only you can carry the light and find some time for yourself, creating a sanctuary, a space where you won't be interrupted. Pull the phone out, turn off the mobile, lock the door and just hang out with yourself. You'll be amazed who you find in there. Don't worry about how quiet and barren it is. If you worry about that, it'd be as silly as worrying about winter. Every winter it gets cold (this is the time to hibernate and reflect). It doesn't mean that spring isn't around the corner and everything won't blossom again.

You need time out to reflect. The Hermit represents a need to look within, and you may even need to change your environment in order to do so.

Your dream may be a story that teaches profound insight. Look deeply at your dream and discover its inner message for you. A meeting with wiser people is at hand. Take time in solitude for learning, contemplation and study.

Wheel of Fortune

Anything is possible. You can make anything you like of your dream. Seeing it in a positive light suggests abundance is forthcoming.

Wheel of Fortune also suggests movement and solutions. It represents motion, so it shows that there's movement happening within your life in regard to the dream, and movement means opportunity or luck. (Luck is being able to recognise an opportunity and *act* on it.)

This card represents a turn for the better. The wheels are in motion, rapid change lies ahead for you. Flow with the changes, there will be a favourable outcome.

Justice

Everyone's definition of justice is different. The justice that you dispense and the justice that is dispensed to you is relative to the individual. With the dream you just had, do what you feel is the most honourable thing to do. If there's an imbalance and it needs to be sorted out, or if you feel you are being dealt a cruel blow, relax and take it on the chin, or deal with it in the best way possible, then leave it alone and move on. Don't look for justice in every situation of your life. You may feel there's no justice at first glimpse, but when you look at the big picture, there seems to be justice in everything.

Justice is there even though it's not perceived as such. Take a court hearing for example. The person who wins feels it's just and the person who loses thinks it's injust. I like the phonetic of justice — just is. We're living in a very artificial world and we are pretty much detached from what is natural, so we don't see justice.

Legal dealings may lie ahead. Adjustments need to be made for success to be assured. Seek the right advice.

Hanged Man

It's time to move on and get back into the game. Stop pondering, stop thinking, get out of your head and back into life. It may be easier to hang about, but don't. Half of you already knows the right thing to do and is ready for action.

One of the biggest things spiritual people need to do is take a good look at reality. Too many people feel that it's better to be somewhere else than here. You're living in the physical to experience every aspect of it. If you are using your life to avoid the physical, then you are missing it. You're missing the point of being here, which is not only to surrender to your direction, but to do things physically and in a real way. Stop being a martyr or victim. Be spiritual, of course, see things from a different point of view and try not to over-analyse, but also do things in the real world. See your life in a different way and also act upon it in a different way.

Can represent an opening up to the God/Goddess. Let the vision of prophesy unfold before you. Dreams of future events yet to happen, even clairvoyant perceptions.

Death

This is a great card. It's a big notice telling you that the genesis of something new is about to happen. Whatever you were dealing with, whatever was affecting you, is over, and something new is coming. It very rarely means that someone is going to die.

Death means completion and endings. The past is dead and buried. Death shows change in some shape or form. Remember, the opposite of life is not death, it is stagnation.

Death can often indicate a birth. A dream symbol of deep cleansing and renewal. Changes that come into play pull you to a new and exciting destiny.

Temperance

Temperance is a strong reminder to get back into balance. If you've been thinking too far to the left, start thinking a little to the right. If you've been drinking too much, then drink a little less. If you've been climbing too many mountains, stay on some flat land.

Temperance is a reminder that there is a lot of strength and power in balance. It's quite easy to sit at a table and eat a three-course meal, empty the last drop of wine, and empty out the salt and sugar shakers, leaving nothing there, but the balance would be leaving the table just a little bit hungry or leaving a glass of wine in the bottle. Balance is about not going overboard so you don't get into problems on your way home; not being so full that you're bloated.

Recognise that excess or fanaticism in anything you believe in, or anything you hold dear to yourself, is debilitating and negative.

Temperance also suggests having a foot in both worlds. Have a foot in the spiritual world, but also be practical. There's no point in being 'heavenly' good and 'earthly' bad. The strongest people are the ones who have got a foot in both worlds. They are very spiritual and mystical, and they're also very practical.

Temperance means transformation, renewal and spirituality will come to the fore. It may be a time to do good deeds. Giving and receiving at a balance is essential now.

This card can indicate divine providence and help from angelic forces. Everyone has a guardian angel, contemplate your problems and hand them over to a higher force for guidance.

The Devil

This is a card which encourages you to find out more about your dark side. If a magnet has a positive and negative end, you can't say that the negative end of the magnet is bad and the positive good, it's simply polarity. You may have dark thoughts and you may be angry and bitchy sometimes, but that's all right, because without sunlight there can't be darkness and without bitterness there can be no sweetness. It's a reminder that there are two polarities and you shouldn't fear the dark side of yourself, rather acknowledge it.

You can have whatever thoughts you like, you can have whatever fantasies you like — do what you like as long as you don't impinge on another individual. Don't feel guilty about being who you are.

Don't let fear run or rule you. If you have a frightening or scary dream, it doesn't mean the event is going to take place, but it does imply trust. You can trust people to be who they are. Be aware of not giving your power away.

The Devil represents a need to release your fears and face your problems with confidence and power. It also implies repressed sexual urges and the need to play more in life. Devil is 'lived' spelt backwards, so you may be suppressing your life force. Acknowledge that there is a dark side to a lot of things.

The Tower

It's time to incinerate all your belief patterns, reinvent yourself or at least have a really good look at yourself. Lightning only strikes once in the same place, so if it's time, it's time. Don't fight it, because next time you are going to be in a different place and it's going to be a different bolt of lightning. This is now, so do it now. When opportunity knocks, answer the door. Don't judge the moment, just appreciate it and whenever you can, reinvent yourself.

Intuition and genius flows when they want to, not when you want them to. Sometimes you are inspired at two o'clock in the morning and you just have to get up. Be natural regardless of what is expected of you.

Use this card as a trigger for intuition, and let your natural genius flow. In a dream the Tower can symbolise quick sudden changes ahead of you. So much so, that once triggered, there is no going back.

The Star

Don't feel you are unappreciated. Stars shine brightly, yet they are not appreciated as much as our central star, the sun. A lot of people are appreciated because they are noisy and more vocal, but you're in the background doing your job silently without noise or fanfare. It's okay to do it that way and feel good about it. You don't have to be out there in the forefront. You know yourself what you've achieved: your stars are burning as bright as the sun, so don't feel you are not appreciated.

Also, if you walk out of step with others, it means you tread on ground that no-one else touches. This card has stars shining in the middle of the day. Well, so be it, they're different. Don't be frightened of your differences.

The Star implies a naturalness. Optimism is now within your reach. Doors previously closed are now open to you. Clarity, vision and new goals are at hand. You are now true to yourself.

The Moon

Don't be worried if someone is trying to block you out or point you in the wrong direction, you have the strength and the power to go beyond that, and it will pass. Eclipses are only momentary, and no matter how much an individual or situation is trying to drag you down, you will be able to go beyond. The situation or the individuals that are trying to keep you in the dark, or block out your sun, really cannot harm you unless you allow yourself to be harmed. The dogs may be howling at the moon, but they can't really hurt it.

Don't worry about the scavengers around you. Don't let the dark forces overpower you. Remember, 'Sticks and stones may break my bones, but names will never hurt me.'

The symbolism of the Moon shows one dog that is wild— the wolf—and one that is tame. It's a representation of the wild and tame sides within all of us.

This card can represent an active dream state where many confusing dreams run together and do not make sense. It is a

**Singer and actor, Barry Crocker has had a
recurring dream since childhood:**

*I saw myself walking along a road when I
noticed a five cent piece on the ground. I stooped
to pick it up, then noticed a 10 cent piece which
I picked up, then a 20 cent piece, and a 50 cent
piece. I continually find money in larger and
larger denominations.*

high trigger for the imagination and can also represent dreams of a psychic nature, or dreams that seem all too real. The symbol of the moon can bring clarity.

The Sun

Bathe in the light of success. A lot of people finish a race and still feel dissatisfied. They don't spend time savouring the moment, instead they ask, what's next? (That was a great dinner, but what's for dessert?) If you draw this card, take time out to celebrate who you are and what you have achieved. Look into the mirror and say, 'Congratulations, you have achieved much in your lifetime,' and pat yourself on the back for every single thing you have achieved. We're not asking you to be egotistical and self-centred, simply honour what you have done for it's quite an achievement.

Also, pat yourself on the back for wanting to understand yourself to the point where you've actually bought this book. That's an achievement in itself. You could have simply let this dream slip through your fingers, yet you've actually gone and done something about it—you are delving.

The Sun is associated with looking at the child within. Celebrate completion, celebrate success. Achievement is not what you do, but who you think you are. Whatever you bring to your dream, bring it to light in a creative way.

Success lies ahead for you. All new beginnings are possible. This card can also imply the ability to laugh, play and have fun in life.

Judgement

Judgement symbolises going beyond limitations and fear. Don't judge yourself to the point where you no longer have the ability or resources to slay the dragon. Whatever problem you were confronting in the dream you will overcome, and your angels and guardian angels will be around to assist you.

This is a very triumphant card. Everyone is looking towards the heavens. Believe in your own ability to travel beyond the forces that are holding you back, and know that you are not alone. For those who believe in guardian angels, they're there, there are also many other people in the world who can help you.

Judgement can also mean sharp focus, and a lot of analysis. It's a resurrection and renewal type card; similar to 'the last judgement'.

A new spiritual path is open to you. There is a need to be less critical and more accepting of yourself and others. A need not to over-analyse your dreams nor be tormented by them.

The World

See if you can work towards making the most of what the world has to offer. Make a point of getting on with people, the elements and situations, instead of finding reasons to be at odds with them. There's a need to once again communicate, and work with, co-exist and understand the people around you. It takes all kinds to make up the world. You may feel that you are the centre of the universe when you draw this card, and everything revolves around you, but it's your job to get along with everything that is around you and co-exist *with* it.

It's a time to accept differences. Time to accept the fact that you do live in the physical world and have to work with physical things.

Your dream involves your awake state in the real world. You are now the master of your destiny.

CHAPTER SEVEN

What a DAY for a DAYDREAM!

The mind of God.
Where does it hide?
Creative impulses of the cosmos,
Where do you abide?
In the depths of your soul
Are boundless energies and
Powerful forces, side by side.

DEEPAK CHOPRA

I've already made the point that everybody is psychic, and that it's just a matter of exercising and intentionally developing this innate ability. At this point, it is important to accept the fact that what has been described throughout the ages as 'extrasensory', 'paranormal' and 'psychic' is really a common human capacity which some have been able to highly develop, while others have chosen to remain mystified. We acquire knowledge through experience, study and research, but we also build knowledge through our intuition. Some call it a hunch, others call it a gut feeling. Whatever it's called, this process plays a necessary part in understanding ourselves.

It is important to develop psychic and intuitive abilities, but it's not necessary to reach a point where we feel we are able to perceive the future. Humans incarnate with free will and we create our world through a multitude of complex decisions— both individually and collectively. As you develop your psychic skills you are actually perceiving possible alternatives. At the moment of perception one can alter the outcome by starting a whole different chain of events.

It is also good to remember that you have choices. Even up to the last moment they are available to you before a decision is finally made. Of course, the more choices you have, the greater your dignity and the better you feel about yourself.

But how do we bring back abundance, personal development and our heart's desires from the dream world into the physical? After all, if we were able to do this at will, what an incredible world we could manifest for ourselves. The key is to know that the conscious mind looks after all the reasoning, focusing and thinking for us, and the subconscious mind deals primarily with experiences, memories, and imagery. All we have to do is create a method where information flows freely from the subconscious into the conscious mind. In this way, fantasy becomes reality.

I once read that many of the greatest ideas were a result of sudden realisation, or the penny dropping rather than as a result of rational thinking. Albert Einstein said: 'Imagination is more important than knowledge, as knowledge is really nothing but experience.'

THE BRAIN CLEAN

If you would like your daydreams to be as creative as possible, one of the first things you should do, I suggest, is have a 'brain clean'. This is done in the same fashion as you would clean a house or a car. Simply remove everything that is cluttering up the space. There is so much 'stuff' hanging around that is of no real use.

Go through and start with anger, especially with petty things in life. The next door neighbour banging the garbage bins every Tuesday morning, getting held up at three sets of red traffic lights in a row, or being served very slowly by someone chewing gum at your local supermarket. Look at it this way: the sound of the rubbish bins are great because they remind you to put your own out. The red lights give you a rest from driving. While you are being served slowly at the supermarket, you may remember an item you forgot to put into your shopping trolley.

This is not to say that you will end up a space cadet who sees love and light in everything. What I'm saying is, avoid as much as possible all the unnecessary baggage that is labelled 'judgement', 'fear', 'frustration', and 'guilt'.

Create for yourself two imaginary buttons in your brain: a delete button and a rewind button. When you have a thought that is not empowering—that blocks your intuition and is totally unproductive—with your mind's eye, press the delete button. Then, rewind to the moment when you had the thought and rethink it in a more positive manner. With the aid of this very simple technique you will find that your creative imagination will become more fruitful and easier to manifest.

Positive daydreaming techniques should never be used to obtain something at another's expense. Nor should they ever be used to control someone's behaviour or to cause them to do something against their will.

There is a law in the East known as the Law of Karma. In the West, it is known as Newton's Third Law of Motion, or cause and effect. Newton's law states: 'For every action there is a justified and corresponding reaction.' In simple terms, this means that your every action causes a reaction. A vibrant example of this is the ripple effect in a pond when you drop a pebble into the water. If you create something in your life that you know has negative energy surrounding it, chances are there will be another jolt or reaction from this scene further down the line.

Increasingly, eliminate as many debilitating thoughts as possible from your daily life. Negative thoughts are an obstacle to the ultimate goal achievement. To reduce negative thought patterns, avoid reading articles and stories of a sensationalised nature in newspapers and magazines. Don't get hooked into the over-dramatised, hyped-up news bulletins that cry out for you to pass judgement and get angry. Instead, consider replacing these with classical music, positive movies or videos, and inspirational novels.

HOME ALONE TIME

Find quiet times for yourself. During the day we seem to find time to work, wash the dog, eat and exercise, but it is possible to neglect the need for creating quality time alone. If we can discipline ourselves to allow a portion of the day to be totally ours, where we can reflect on who we are, where we are going, what we are doing here, we will be better equipped to understand what we *don't* want in our lives, and then by the process of elimination, what we *do* want in our lives.

Finally, each and every day, avoid going to sleep without doing one thing that makes you happy. No matter how miserable you may feel on a particular occasion, step out of that mode, even if it's only for five minutes and give yourself a laugh. This can be done quite easily by listening to some music, replaying a small part of a favourite movie, re-reading a chapter out of a book, or perhaps learning how to juggle.

This simple act shows there is always room for happiness, which can be created under the most adverse circumstances and which can be manifested at the drop of a hat. Once the conscious mind sees that it is totally rational to be happy, you will not feel any apprehension.

CREATIVE DAYDREAMING

Creative daydreaming is the technique of using our imagination to create what we want in our lives. There is nothing at all new, strange, or unusual about this. It is our innate power of imagination—our basic creative power of the universe which we constantly use—whether we are aware of it or not.

It's important to visualise our daydreams in a positive manner or with positive intentions. Think about the last time you really wanted something. Maybe it was a holiday in the sun. Firstly, you visualised the holiday, then you went to your travel agent and picked up a brochure to further enhance the mental image. You saved your money and arranged time off. Finally, you were on your way, without consciously thinking how brilliantly you brought your dream to reality.

Unfortunately, it is also possible to daydream in a negative fashion. It is possible to develop deep-seated negative concepts of life, unconsciously expecting limitation and difficulties.

By using the positive side of the imagination — daydreams — in a more conscious way, any daydream can help to create what you truly want in life: more love, fulfilment, enjoyment, satisfying relationships, rewarding work, self-expression, health, beauty, prosperity, inner peace and harmony.

There is a basic technique for consciously creating ideas or mental pictures in your mind, for using your imagination to create a clear image of something you wish to manifest. This process involves continuing to focus on the idea regularly, giving it positive energy until it becomes reality. You might imagine yourself with a new home, or a new job, or having a beautiful relationship, or feeling calm and serene, or perhaps with a happier outlook to life. Any day is a good day for a daydream. Just sit or lie quietly (always make sure your spine is straight), close your eyes if you wish to, and mentally picture the sequence of events you would like to materialise. Then set about bringing your daydream to reality. If it's a new car you desire, visualise yourself happily driving. See yourself pleased with the choice you've made and with a feeling of contentment, knowing that what you are driving you own and can afford to run and maintain. In this way you are not limiting yourself to any particular car, but the car that is ultimately the most suitable for you.

My good friend, author and philosopher Stuart Wilde, says:

A lot of people do a lot of daydreaming and the mind knows the largest percentage component of a daydream is pure fantasy. So, if you believe that you have no physical ability or the skills to achieve the fantasy, your mind knows that this component isn't there and begins to disenfranchise the whole of your daydreams.

Always daydream heroically. There has to be power. Real positive daydreaming, or critical thinking as I like to call it, about one's life, occurs when you begin to dream heroically, with passion, with so much intent and desire that your mind differentiates between mental masturbation and those big dreams that our minds and spirit can believe in.

So dream the impossible dream. Give it the power and the intensity a heroic dream deserves so that your mind understands this is your quest.

WHAT MAKES IT TICK?

So just how does positive daydreaming, or creative daydreaming, work? The scientific world is beginning to discover what metaphysical and spiritual teachers have long known—that our physical universe is governed by energy. It is not just an objective world governed by mathematical laws. It is not simply by measuring and observing that we can understand reality. There is more to it. Intuition and creative thinking are woven into the fibre of our existence.

It was American author Shakti Gawain, with whom I've had the pleasure of working, who popularised the technique of positive daydreaming with her inspirational book entitled *Creative Visualisation*, first published in 1979. Shakti Gawain explains it this way:

Physically, we are all energy, and everything within and around us is made up of energy. This energy is vibrating at different rates of speed, and therefore has different qualities, from finer to denser.

All forms of energy are interrelated and can affect one another.

One law of energy is this: energy of a certain quality or vibration tends to attract energy of a similar quality and vibration.

Thought and feelings have their own magnetic energy which attract energy of a similar nature. We can see this principle at work, for instance, when we 'run into someone' we've just been thinking about.

How often have you been going to telephone someone and shortly before you do they ring you? Similarly, you may happen to pick up a book which contains exactly the information you need at that particular time.

QUICK AS A FLASH

Thought is a quick, light, mobile form of energy. It manifests instantaneously. When we create something in our lives, we have always created it first in thought form. A thought or idea always precedes manifestation or physical use of a certain thing. 'I think I need to laugh and relax so I'm going to the movies to watch a comedy.' Thoughts such as these always precede the action of travelling to a cinema. They are like blueprints and plans of action that enable us to physically achieve through action, the desired result—relaxation and laughter.

Marshall Lever, prolific author, says:

I'm convinced that I can change the direction of anyone's life by helping them to change the direction of their thinking. This statement is very simple, but applying it requires a tremendous amount of discipline and personal dedication by the individual who wants to make that change.

Remember your thoughts and words can be in perfect order, but if they are not supported by positive action you have taken one step forward and four backward!

I encourage you to spend a greater amount of time positive daydreaming. It's not an indication that you are becoming a lazy person. It's a conscious desire for realignment and movement to the next creative stage or adventure in your life.

IT'S HALF FULL

Recently, I watched a program on television where two professors in the USA had surveyed people who were over 100 years old. Their purpose was to see if there was a common denominator amongst them and if this common denominator could be utilised by all of us to live longer.

They found four key similarities or, should I say, detectable common threads. These were:

1. The ability to handle grief. As you can imagine living to a ripe old age, one would experience a large number of family and friends moving on.
2. They currently had a purpose in life, either a job, community work and/or businesses. In essence, a reason to keep living.
3. They were adaptable and flexible in their attitudes. Put simply, if in the past they went to work in a horse and buggy and now they have to use a motorcar, that was fine. If they used to shop at a corner store but now they have to shop in a big supermarket, that was fine too.

4. The most important common thread experienced by these individuals was that they displayed high levels of optimism. When asked about the environment, it was a matter of no worries, the scientists and the 'greenies' will work something out. The economy? No problems. The economists and accountants will come up with a system. Their health? No problems. The incredible medical profession and holistic practitioners will find an answer between them.

The lesson here is, we can survive a lot longer with an optimistic approach to life, believing that with application and intention we can solve any problems that will emerge. As John Lennon once said, 'There are no problems, there are only solutions.'

Marshall Lever wrote the following about optimism:

Personally, I have always equated positive and negative with acid and alkaline. Nutritionally we need 20 per cent of acid foods in our life and 80 per cent of alkaline. I believe life is the same; we need at least 20 per cent acid to maintain a balance. Frankly, I have found that it is easier for a negative individual to change acid into alkaline in their life than for a positive person to add some acid from the unknown.

However, each of these goals can be attained quite easily. It only takes a change in attitude. I know ... that sounds too simple. But the kind of 'change in attitude' I am talking about has a slight twist to it.

Dream more than others think is practical! Those of us who dream are actually creating our tomorrows. I am acquainted with a lot of dreamers and the ones I truly enjoy the most are the ones everyone else thinks are a little wacky or eccentric. Not long ago, I read an entire book about the problems of being a dreamer. Frankly, after reading this I was truly glad that I have not been 'practical' as exemplified by this author, who I am sure has each and every day of his life planned up until the last moment.

Dreamers are usually happy; they enjoy life and are definitely willing to laugh at themselves. I once knew a dreamer who never did a practical thing in his long and joyful lifetime. Boy, do I miss him!

Care more than others think is wise! Risk more than others think is safe! Expect more than others think is possible! Dream more than others think is practical! Then we will truly begin to see life as half full rather than half empty!

THE HEALTH CONSCIOUS DAYDREAMER

Medical science is fast becoming aware of the power of the mind in warding off disease, and staying young and vibrant. Evidence is growing to indicate that a strong, positive mental attitude—regardless of the hardships we face—can stave off disease and help us lead a long and healthy life. 'It is part of the cure to wish to be cured,' is a famous old saying.

One of the unfortunate aspects of health education is that it tends to make us more aware of our weaknesses than of our strengths. By focusing our attention and concerns on things that can go wrong, we tend to develop a one-sided view of the human body and mind, regarding it as a ready receiver for all sorts of illnesses.

I believe the most important lesson of all in health education is to understand that the human body is a robust mechanism, capable of attending to most of its needs and that the mind plays a dominant role in all health-restoring processes. A will to

TV host, Ronnie Burns' dream:

*I'm standing in a room and slowly peeling off
my clothes. I take off the good suit I'm wearing,
but I find there's another suit beneath it. Again,
I disrobe, only to find that I'm wearing another
suit and another.*

combat the illness, along with other positive emotions, such as those already mentioned, are biochemical realities that affect the environment of medical care.

It is now well accepted that depression is a cause of physical illness leading to a deterioration of the immune system and the onset of chronic disease symptoms. It is a striking fact that liberation from depression produces an almost automatic boost in the number of disease-fighting immune cells.

Remember, a positive mind keeps us healthy. This is no mystical concept — it really does work. If you want better health, visualise yourself completely accepting where you are right now and know that your body is making the right decisions to keep you functioning at an optimum level. Know that your body is wise enough to understand that desire for self preservation and realise that whatever you are experiencing is part of that goal of survival, even though it might not be apparent to you and in itself may seem the opposite.

Once you get into the space of right place, right experience and right time, then you can move on and visualise yourself becoming stronger physically and emotionally. However, it must come from the point of view of where you are right now is perfect and totally acceptable to you, rather than that you are not in good health and you need to get healthier.

Some of the most remarkable healing stories on record are those which have involved positive daydreaming, particularly in the area of alternative cancer therapy. It is possible to eat only the healthiest foods available, drink the most purified water and exercise every day, but not outlive a smoking, junk food addict, if one is continually stressed out by negative thoughts or ego-related fears.

THE NON-INFRINGING
DAYDREAMER

The majority of daydreams have a happy ending for the dreamer. They take on a fairytale-like story situation where things are resolved and satisfactory conclusions are achieved. For this reason, I encourage you to daydream as often as your heart desires. However, one of the most important rules you must consider about daydreams is that you must do your utmost not to infringe on another human being.

Most daydreams have desire in them. You must do your utmost to discipline yourself so that your desires don't infringe on another human being. Once you can do this, you remove the one obstacle that may prevent your dreams coming true, and that is guilt.

Consider the following example: Imagine a man working away in his backyard. Suddenly he finds himself looking over the fence at his next door neighbour who is washing his 20-foot yacht and helping to connect it up to the family's brand new Rodeo Jeep. His children are running around picking up life jackets and his wife looks like she should be on a catwalk, with a magnificent figure, the latest hairstyle, a brilliant smile and flashing white teeth. This man finds himself starting to daydream and wishing that it was his life. He'd love a boat like that, a house like that, children like that, and even more, he'd love a wife like that! If he can't control his thoughts, he may even want the very woman concerned, even though the couple next door are friends, and he knows that they have worked hard to create the life they have together.

Daydreams such as this can clearly be an infringement on others, and are best avoided at all times. In this hypothetical example, the man imposed his wants on the entire family next door. He infringed on their whole existence. What someone else has is theirs. Always imagine your own success. Your own achievements. Your own happiness. Your own spiritual fulfilment. Imagine your own boat and your own family. If you do find yourself jealously daydreaming about someone else's achievements and their good fortune, while you are experiencing a phase of loss or misfortune, discipline yourself to overcome these negative thought processes and get on with creating your own life.

Non-infringement concepts are not the easiest to grasp. In the case we have just shown, if the family next door were to pick up on the man's thoughts, their entire relationship with him may change. They may not feel comfortable around this man, feeling he is jealous of their achievements.

Daydream by all means, but avoid infringing on others! This is a message that cannot be stressed enough. If you find yourself gravitating towards an infringing daydream such as the one described, remove the neighbours, their house and yacht, their entire image. Go to an imaginary place and create your own yacht, your own beautiful wife/husband, your own home and kids, your very own life. When daydreams become guilt-ridden, there is no fun and no long-term success. Try to achieve your own personal goals.

Glynn Braddy, health researcher, explains infringement this way:

When positive daydreaming becomes a projection that requires a specific decision or action by others, then it becomes an infringement on them.

It removes their right to make their own decisions to develop in the context of their own evolution, ideals and goals.

Further, if positive daydreaming involves another person and one imagines them in a context of having made a mistake — whether it is by being alone, unwell or experiencing lack — the presumption of error on their part is a judgement of their right to evolve as an individual separate from the expectations of others.

Besides, to look at something and declare it to be a mistake ... or to be something to be changed is to deny that we create what we experience for our highest good. Our highest good is evolution and is not always convenient.

The key to positive daydreaming is to emphasise your ideals: creativity, nurturing, philosophical depth and the celebration of life in the physical. Keep to your ideals and allow others to find theirs free of your projections on them.

Ponder the following example and perceive the infringing projection. I have a goal that a film script I have written is accepted by producers. I see these producers reading my script and they love it and they're now contacting me to ask me to do the film. They're tearing up all the other people's scripts and it's now going ahead; they've chosen me. No matter how nice it sounds for me, the fact is this desire infringes on the producer's right to choose the best script and creates a situation that denies him or her the exploration of their creativity. By choosing mine it is implicit that they deny others.

On the other hand, ponder the next example and see if you can recognise the difference. I see the producers contacting me to ask me to work for them in the capacity of a scriptwriter. I am working at my computer, the phones are ringing, I am busy and feeling abundant. I am now in a situation whereby I imagine myself in the context of my goals and ideals.

A positive daydream is one that does not ask for anything to occur around anyone else's free will; one that is contained by our ideals and where we do not seek to infringe on the right of another individual to make choices, except as an individual in their own right.

PERSONAL INFRINGEMENTS

It is very easy to infringe on your own evolution by reducing yourself to a point where you imagine a certain situation occurring. By trying to construct the details to a point where they are so airtight and specific, it limits your full and unknown potential.

Here is an example. You may visualise that you're getting $20, but it may cause you to miss out on $20,000, or if you visualise $20,000 you may miss out on $20 million. So the idea should always be to keep your dream focused on abundance, rather than limitations. Specifics in a visualisation or positive daydream can be a limitation.

GOING BACK
TO THE FUTURE

The purpose of a daydream is to achieve; to manifest whatever part of the daydream is useful to you. This is positive daydreaming at work. You can also use daydreaming very successfully to go back into your past and change your thinking about events which have affected you emotionally. This is a very useful technique which can improve the way you feel about yourself.

Take the following hypothetical situation: Remember when you were at school, you were sitting in the classroom and you liked one of the boys/girls in the room, you passed a note along to that person but the teacher saw you and forced you to read that note out in front of everyone. This episode embarrassed you greatly and you were apprehensive about putting your feelings on paper from then on.

Using your daydream techniques, wander back into your past, confront this thought that continues to trouble you, and rationalise it. Okay, it wasn't a happy experience, and it has cost you a few friends. Imagine yourself instead of reading out the content of the note, thinking quickly and reading out, 'This is a really great history lesson. Mr Smith is a great teacher isn't he?' Feel yourself gaining strength, and change your thinking towards this episode with a positive, less embarrassing outcome. See yourself feeling better gradually.

In this way, daydreaming can be used not only to achieve your goals in life, but it can also be used to subtly change your memory of what has passed.

SOULMATES FOR DAYDREAMERS

Most of us desire quality relationships. Some of us want to connect with soulmates. Others are quite happy to leave all the bonding to the physical. It is possible to create greater happiness in your relationships with positive daydreams, by focusing on the things you would like in them.

See yourself full of anticipation on your way home, because you know there is someone waiting for you. See yourself opening the door, knowing that there is actually someone there and that you are about to embark on long conversations about your day, your feelings and aspirations. See yourself about to do all your favourite leisure time activities. You are content because you know that there is someone who shares the same interests and is about to do them with you. Finally, see yourself in that last minute before sleep overtakes you at night feeling safe and secure because someone you love is next to you.

The perception here is that you see yourself content and you understand this feeling of contentment because you are in a supportive relationship. The important thing is not to go to the point where you actually see the individual that is the other half of your relationship. Just know that you are in a relationship that is satisfying without actually projecting what the other person is going to look like and who they are. Allow the person who is going to best provide this feeling of satisfaction to come into your life without you making any judgements or having any preconceived ideas. See yourself in a balance when it comes to a relationship without necessarily demanding that you should know in advance who's going to assist you in creating the balance.

Finally, it is important to realise that all your fantasies belong to you. Do not feel guilty about fantasising, even when you have an erotic fantasy with an imaginary dream lover or lovers. As long as you don't infringe on another individual there is no thought-crime.

MANIFESTING THE DREAM

To best explain the energy that is required to manifest a dream or a creative daydream, I would like to share a parable that illustrates the point perfectly. There was a Chinese emperor's son who could not get out of his bed or walk. As the young boy was to be the next emperor, the imperial court was alarmed and physicians were summoned to see if, through their knowledge, they could make the boy walk again. They all came but to no avail. Magicians, psychics and healers of all descriptions were then commanded to visit the palace and do what they could to make the young boy walk again. A few years passed and still the boy did not stir from his bed. There came a point where no-one even bothered to try any more, dismissing the situation as impossible.

One morning, while walking through his garden, the emperor looked at a pond surrounded by a small haze of mist and recalled how as a child he once was assisted by an old hermit who lived in a forest in the northern part of the kingdom. Many of his subjects believed the hermit was really a sage; a wizard beyond human comprehension. The emperor thought, why not? And as the hermit never ventured out of his forest, the emperor mounted an expedition and took his son to the very spot where the sage last appeared.

Calling out for the hermit was useless. So the emperor left the boy by the small lake and retreated to a clearing some distance away and made a camp. That evening, just before sunset, an old man appeared before the young emperor-to-be and looked down and smiled. The child looked up, more curious than scared. The old man picked the child up and walked into the lake. When he was about waist high in the water the old man dropped the boy in the water and held his head down.

The child kicked and splattered and pushed until he was exhausted and there was no further movement. The old man lifted him out of the water and threw him on the bank. The boy began to vomit the lake water, and cough and splutter. When he regained his composure he screamed at the old man.

'My father will kill you, you old fool. Why did you do that?'

The old man said, 'Do you remember how much you wanted another breath of air? Do you remember the moment before you exhaled the last mouthful of air and how you would've given up anything, knocked over anyone in your way, taken on anyone just to have one more mouthful of air? Well, when you want to walk as much as you wanted the breath of air you desired in that final moment before you passed out, then and only then will you walk again.'

The boy looked at the old man as if he understood. But within seconds he found himself back in the water, deep enough not to be able to reach the surface. Once again, when he passed out, he was unceremoniously thrown on the bank.

Again the old sage said to him, 'When you want to walk as much as you want the next breath of air, you will walk.'

Once again, before the child had the chance to understand the full meaning of the words, he found himself back in the water, gasping for air, but this time he walked out on his own two feet.

The point here is that when you truly want to manifest something in your life, the way you desire to take the next breath of air which is the only thing between life and death, that's when you'll get it. It really has to be that important to you for it to work.

Creative daydreaming, visualisation techniques, positive mental attitudes and repeating affirmations a thousand times over are as useful as a flea in a dogshow if they are not accompanied by absolute, dedicated, focused passion. It's okay to fantasise to your heart's content as long as you realise that it's no different to going to a movie. You are creating an event, a set of circumstances in your mind. You are really doing no more than observing.

The human mind, if it so desires, can do anything, go anywhere and create anything at will. If the object of this experience is just to fantasise, then well and good. But if you want to go beyond the fantasy and actually turn imagination into reality, then a few simple techniques need to be considered. Look around, meditate and be sure of what you want, work out what it's going to take to get it, and don't let anyone bump you off the path.

In other words, you can't help someone until you know what they want. If someone walks up to you and asks how to get to Main Street from here it's easy to direct them: turn left, take the third street on your right and there it is. How do you answer if someone walks up to you and says, 'I want to get somewhere and change my location but I'm not sure where I want to go.' What direction can you offer? You can only help them if they know where they want to end up.

Everything in this dimension has a price. I mean everything. Given that this is the case, seriously look at the cost of this quest and make up your mind if you're willing to pay it. The cost could be being called stubborn, pig-headed, irrational, inconsiderate, ungrateful. It doesn't have to be a monetary cost; it doesn't have to cost you thousands of dollars or your house and lifestyle. It can be merely measured in the way you are perceived by others. It could be at the cost of losing friends. The cost could perhaps be the realisation that you will never compete in a sporting event or travel in an aeroplane. Once the cost is ascertained, and you want it as much as your next breath of air, pay it, as the young emperor to be did. You ask what did it cost him? He ceased to be the focus of massive imperial attention. He ceased to be different. He became as normal as a prince could be growing up in the palace with all the duties that are connected to the office.

THE AWAKENING

The idea I want to leave you with is quite simple. Imagine that dreaming is like going on a holiday. While on holidays, two obvious ways of remembering your experience are to take your own photographs or buy postcards. The postcards are an expression of how someone else sees your holiday. The photographs place you in the picture and the experience.

With any self improvement or self help information it really doesn't matter how much we study the contents and devote ourselves to its wisdom, we will never get to the point where we fully understand the meaning of life. What does happen to us is that, when we are ready, we come to understand what has meaning in our lives. It is a continual journey of conscious expanding and contracting adventures.

Dreams, I believe, are our guiding light when we need a blueprint of the real picture. They provide a subtle hint on how to overcome challenges that we have created to make our lives not only more meaningful, not only more interesting, but as unique as our fingertips.

Marcia Hines

As a child living in Boston, I remember having a recurring dream. A huge monster was chasing me through marshlands. I was running with other people when they all began to lay down. The monster rolled over and squashed them into the marsh. It wasn't able to topple me over though because I remained upright, refusing to lay down like the others around me.

FURTHER READING

Glynn Braddy
Glynn Braddy is a true metaphysician and alchemist who has the unsurpassed ability to continually facilitate transformation in others. He lives in Sydney, Australia, and can be contacted on (02) 9977 8433 (local)/(612)9977 8433 (international).

Deepak Chopra
Deepak Chopra is the bestselling author of 18 books and Director of Educational Programs at the Chopra Center for Well Being in La Jolla, California. Phone (619) 551 7147.

Karen Downes and Judith White
Karen Downes and Judith White, co-authors of six aromatherapy books, are regarded by many as foremost authorities in this field. Phone (03) 9486 9688 (local)/(613) 9486 9688 (international).

Wayne Dyer
Wayne Dyer, the Father of Motivation, has written 15 internationally acclaimed books. He lives in Florida with his family. Phone (954) 561 0701.

Louise Hay
Louise Hay is a teacher and lecturer in the field of personal growth, and author of 15 books. She lives in California. If you have any enquiries phone Hay House on (800) 654 5126.

Marshall N. Lever

Marshall is a well-respected metaphysician. He is now enjoying a well-earned retirement, writing books in his spare time. Write to PO Box 93, Gerringong, NSW, 2534.

Denise Linn

Denise Linn is a healer and author who has a unique understanding of the spiritual ways of indigenous people around the world. She lives in Seattle, Washington. She can be reached by fax on (206) 528 2469.

David A. Phillips

David is the author of 15 books. He is best remembered for his international bestseller, *Secrets of the Inner Self*. He passed away in 1993.

Trevor Ravenscroft

Trevor Ravenscroft studied the history of metaphysics. His bestselling book *The Spear of Destiny* takes us to the very heart of mythology for the betterment of humankind and its future. He passed away in 1990.

Stuart Wilde

Stuart Wilde, author and lecturer, delivers a clear message in a humorous and controversial style. He has written 11 books and resides in London. You can contact his website on http://www.powersource.com/wilde or phone (02) 95976297 (local)/ (505) 758 0500 (international).

OTHER BOOKS BY
LEON NACSON

Aromatherapy for Lovers and Dreamers
(co-authored by Karen Downes and Judith White)
Aromatherapy for Lovers and Dreamers gives a detailed account of
how to use essential oils to awaken the lover and dreamer in
us.

Aromatherapy for Medication and Contemplation
(co-authored by Karen Downes and Judith White)
Aromatherapy for Meditation and Contemplation shows readers how
they can use essential oils to enhance meditation and contemplation in their lives.

Dyer Straight
Dyer Straight provides straight answers from Wayne Dyer on
personal growth, self-help, relationships and abundance.

Cards, Stars and Dreams
(co-authored by Matthew Favaloro)
Cards, Stars and Dreams combines tarot, astrology and dreams
in a practical way so readers can use it to find inner guidance.

Deepak Chopra's World of Infinite Possibilities
In *Deepak Chopra's World of Infinite Possibilities* Deepak discusses
all areas of his work in a question/answer format.

Leon Nacson was born in Alexandra, Egypt, to Greek parents. He is the founder and publisher of *The Planet* newspaper, a well-established publication that deals with environmental, healing and personal development issues. He has also facilitated seminars and workshops throughout Australia for such notable individuals as Louise Hay, Denise Linn, Shakti Gawain, Stuart Wilde and Deepak Chopra. Leon's intention was to write a book that is easy to understand, simple in content and sprinkled with his unique brand of irreverent humour.